The Ten Commandments Of Friendship

Sisterhood Principles Every Woman Should Live By

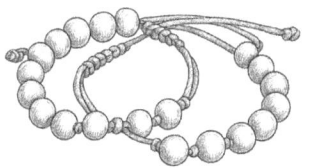

Marla A. McCarthy

The Ten Commandments of Friendship: Sisterhood Principles Every Woman Should Live By. Copyright © 2025 by Marla A. McCarthy

All rights reserved.

No part of this publication may be copied, stored in a retrieval system, or transmitted in any form or by any means—electronic, mechanical, photocopying, recording, or otherwise—without the prior written permission of the publisher, except in the case of brief quotations used in reviews, articles, or scholarly works.

This book is intended for informational and inspirational purposes only. It is not a substitute for professional advice. The author and publisher make no guarantees regarding the results individuals may experience from the information provided.

For permissions, inquiries, or bulk orders, please contact: rlspublishing@gmail.com

Published by
The Real Life Series Publishing Co., LLC
All rights reserved.
Printed in the United States of America
www.thereallifeseries.com

First Edition: July 2025
ISBN: 979-8-9989754-4-8
Library of Congress Control Number: 2025911177

Scripture Acknowledgments:

Scripture quotations marked (KJV) are from the King James Version of the Bible.

Scripture quotations marked (ESV) are from The Holy Bible, English Standard Version® (ESV), copyright © 2001 by Crossway, a publishing ministry of Good News Publishers. Used by permission. All rights reserved.

Scripture quotations marked (GNT) are from the Good News Translation® (Today's English Version, Second Edition) © 1992 American Bible Society. Used by permission. Scripture quotations marked (MSG) are from The Message, copyright © 1993, 1994, 1995, 1996, 2000, 2001, 2002. Used by permission of NavPress Publishing Group. All rights reserved.

Scripture quotations marked (NIV) are from the HOLY BIBLE, NEW INTERNATIONAL VERSION®. Copyright © 1973, 1978, 1984 by the International Bible Society. Used by permission of Zondervan. All rights reserved. "NIV" and "New International Version" are trademarks registered in the U.S. Patent and Trademark Office by the International Bible Society.

Scripture quotations marked (AMP) are from The Amplified® Bible, copyright © 1954, 1958, 1962, 1964, 1965, 1987 by The Lockman Foundation. Used by permission. (www.Lockman.org)

Publisher Contact:
The Real Life Series Publishing Co., LLC
Email: rlspublishing@gmail.com

DEDICATION

To my sisters, Gena, Kendra, and Amber, and to our (big) little brother, Michael:

Your presence in my life has been a divine gift. Thank you for your unwavering love, your laughter, your encouragement, and the deep-rooted connection that only siblings and lifelong friends can understand.

Our shared memories, honest conversations, and even our quiet moments together have shaped me in more ways than words can express. Your prayers and support have been the quiet strength behind many of my greatest steps forward. This book is, in many ways, a reflection of what you've taught me about life, loyalty, compassion, and showing up for each other, even when life gets messy.

To the few remarkable women who have stood beside me through the storms, who never walked away when things were hard, who stayed when staying was hard, I see you. I cherish you. Your sisterhood has been a lifeline. Thank you for holding space for me even when I couldn't find the words to ask for help. Thank you for praying for me and loving me through my most vulnerable seasons.

To every woman reading this, especially the sisters and friends who give without keeping score, who love fiercely, and who continue to show up with grace and grit: This book is for you.

May these words remind you of the beauty and sacredness of sisterhood, the strength found in real friendship, and the healing power of being fully seen and fully loved. I pray these pages inspire women everywhere to treasure the gift of having one another on this journey, and to never take for granted the power of a loyal heart and a listening ear.

With all my love and deepest gratitude,
—*Marla*

TABLE OF CONTENTS

Introduction | 1
Acquaintances vs. Friends | 9
40 Qualities of a Good Friend | 13
40 Traits of a Toxic Friend | 19
I - Honor Each Other's Boundaries | 25
II - Celebrate Her Wins Like They're Your Own | 31
III - Protect Her Kindness, Don't Take Advantage | 39
IV - Speak the Truth in Love | 45
V - Practice Compassion Over Criticism | 53
XI - Let Go of Control and Let Her Be Herself | 59
XII - Show Up When It Matters Most | 67
XIII - Keep Her Name Safe | 75
IX - Listen to Hear, Not to Respond | 83
X - Apologize Often, Forgive Freely | 93
Conclusion | 105

THE TEN COMMANDMENTS OF FRIENDSHIP
Introduction

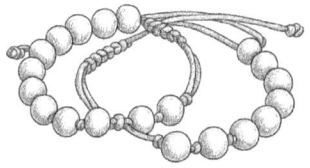

Friendship... is not something you learn in school. But if you haven't learned the meaning of friendship, you really haven't learned anything. —Muhammad Ali

The Friendship We All Crave

There's something deeply sacred about friendship. Not the surface-level, social-media kind. Not the "I-like-your-posts-but-don't-know-your-heart" kind. I'm talking about the kind of friendship that holds your hand through heartbreak. The kind that prays you through a storm. The type that rejoices with you when your dreams come true, and stays close when they don't.

Over the years, I've come to see that real, lasting friendship is not an accident. It is an intentionally cultivated relationship built on trust, truth, and time. In today's world of digital connection and emotional isolation, many of us are starving for the real thing.

As a wife of over 25 years, mom of seven, certified Master Life and Empowerment Coach, and woman of deep faith, I've learned this truth: You can know many people and still feel completely alone. You can be surrounded by busyness, family, success, even love, and still long for the kind of soul-deep connection that only true friendship can bring.

I've walked through seasons of joy and breakthrough

but also deep grief, betrayal, disappointment, and devastating loss. My mother passed away very early in my motherhood and marital journey. My husband suffered the life-threatening condition of having multiple strokes.

I've experienced having children who have suffered injuries and battled serious health challenges. I've also had to balance being a caretaker, daughter, sister, aunt, niece, cousin, friend, businesswoman, coach, and community member. And through it all, the few friends who stood by me, the ones who prayed with me, cried with me, laughed with me, and stayed when it was hard, reminded me just how valuable friendship truly is.

Why This Book Matters Now

We live in a time when many women are burned out, heartbroken, and doing their best to keep it all together. We manage families, careers, businesses, and ministries, but inside, many of us feel disconnected and unseen.

We scroll past smiling faces online but quietly grieve the absence of real connection. We've experienced friend wounds, ghosting, comparison, envy, and silent struggles. We don't just need more friends. We need healed hearts and healthy relationships.

That's why this book is more than just principles; it's a movement toward reclaiming friendship as a divine part of a full, faith-filled life. *The Ten Commandments of Friendship: Sisterhood Principles Every Woman Should Live By* is here to help you:

- Recognize and heal from friendship wounds
- Build more profound, more authentic relationships
- Learn how to forgive, support, and connect even

through life's most challenging seasons
- Embrace God's design for a healthy community and sisterhood

A Faith-Filled Framework for Friendship

Sisterhood is worth building and, in some cases, rebuilding. Friendship isn't just a bonus in life; it's a lifeline. In a world where women often carry so much: motherhood, careers, caregiving, dreams, disappointments. True friendship becomes a divine gift and a critically important part of our journey.

Building and maintaining meaningful connections in adulthood isn't always easy. Between busy schedules, past hurts, and changing seasons, friendships can drift, break, or never even get off the ground. That's why this book was created, for you.

Inside, you'll find a faith-filled roadmap to the kind of sisterhood your soul craves: loyal, honest, joy-filled, and rooted in God's truth. Blending practical coaching with timeless biblical wisdom, The 10 Commandments of Friendship walks you through ten powerful principles to help you form and sustain authentic, life-giving relationships that last.

The Bible doesn't shy away from friendship; in fact, it celebrates it. Proverbs 17:17 reminds us that "a friend loves at all times," and Jesus Himself calls us friends (John 15:15). If God values friendship so deeply, we should too.

Whether you're seeking to heal from toxic connections, deepen the bonds you already have, or bravely step into new friendships, this book will guide you with grace, honesty, and purpose. Let's build the kind of sisterhood that makes life richer and our faith stronger, together.

The Ten Commandments Of Friendship

A Call to Rise Higher

This isn't about being a *perfect* friend. It's about being a *present, prayerful, and purposeful* one. No one expects you to have it all figured out. What matters is that you're willing to grow, willing to ask God to shape you into the kind of woman who brings light, love, and faith into the lives of those around her.

Maybe you've been hurt by friendships in the past. Perhaps you've struggled with loneliness, comparison, or a lack of trust. Or maybe you're in a season where you're craving deeper connection. Wherever you are, know this: friendship is not just a gift; it's a calling.

So whether you're curled up on the couch with this book and a cup of coffee, reading alongside your best friend, or gathering with a circle of women hungry for authentic sisterhood, I invite you to open your heart. Be honest. Be expectant. And let God gently guide you to become the kind of friend you were created to be, one who uplifts, encourages, and reflects His love in every relationship.

What You'll Find in This Book

In the pages ahead, you'll find:

- Real-life stories, wisdom, and encouragement
- Uplifting quotes + relevant Bible verses
- Reflection questions and journaling prompts
- Coaching tips to help you grow in each area
- Reminders that you are not alone, and you are not too late to build lasting friendships.

In this book, I'll walk you through *The Ten Commandments of Friendship*. Again, don't worry, this isn't about being perfect. It's about learning how to show up with love, wisdom, and maturity in our relationships.

Before we discuss the commandments, we'll begin with foundational wisdom that will help you reflect on your current circle and define what friendship really means in this season of your life.

You'll explore:

1. *Acquaintances vs. Friends:* Learn how to stop calling everyone your friend and start identifying who's truly walking with you.
2. *40 Qualities of a Good Friend:* So you can become one and recognize one.
3. *40 Traits of a Toxic Friend*: Because awareness is the first step toward healing, protecting your peace, and setting boundaries.

Then, we'll explore the principles that will help you build and nurture genuine relationships in today's fast-paced, filter-heavy world.

Each chapter includes:

- Coaching prompts to help you grow in that area
- Biblical wisdom and scriptures to root your friendships in truth
- Reflection questions to deepen your self-awareness and healing
- Sisterhood-style encouragement that feels like a warm hug and a loving nudge

Here's a Glimpse of What You'll Discover:

The Ten Commandments Of Friendship

1. *Honor Each Other's Boundaries* - You'll learn how to respect space, time, privacy, and emotional limits because in healthy friendships you allow one another to breathe. Boundaries don't push people away; they protect the relationship.
2. *Celebrate Her Wins Like They're Your Own* - We'll confront jealousy and comparison head-on and practice becoming the kind of woman who claps for others without shrinking herself.
3. *Protect Her Kindness, Don't Take Advantage* - You'll learn how to give and receive love without imbalance, guilt, or entitlement. This chapter will show you how to avoid unintentionally draining your friends.
4. *Speak the Truth in Love* - Hard conversations don't have to hurt, they can heal. Here, we'll talk about honesty, accountability, and being a friend who lovingly tells the truth without tearing someone down.
5. *Practice Compassion Over Criticism* - You'll discover how empathy builds deeper bonds. This chapter will help you respond to your friends' struggles with softness and grace, not judgment.
6. *Let Go of Control and Let Her Be Herself* - True friends don't manipulate. This chapter will help you release the pressure to fix, change, or control others, and embrace the gift of acceptance.
7. *Show Up When It Matters Most* - You'll learn the power of presence, especially in life's most challenging seasons. When your friend is grieving, overwhelmed, or celebrating, we don't ghost; we show up.
8. *Keep Her Name Safe When She's Not in the Room* - We'll deal with gossip, secrecy, and the temptation to "vent" at someone else's expense. This chapter teaches loyalty, confidentiality, and integrity.

9. *Listen to Hear, Not to Respond* - This one's all about communication. You'll learn how to become a safe space and truly hear the heart of your sister-friends.
10. *Apologize Often, Forgive Freely* - No friendship is perfect. This final chapter will help you repair what's been broken, release bitterness, and pursue reconciliation with wisdom and grace.

A Movement, Not Just a Message

This book isn't just something to read. It's something to live, and it's something to share.

- Use it in your women's group, Bible study, or book club
- Host a "Friendship Circle" or "Healing Sisterhood" workshop
- Pair it with the companion journal or retreat workbook (coming soon!)
- Follow along at @momlifewithmarla and share your #FriendshipCommandments story

Together, we're starting a movement of women who know how to love deeply, walk wisely, and grow stronger in faith and sisterhood.

You were never meant to do life alone. And you don't have to anymore. Let's rediscover what it means to love well, forgive often, and show up for one another through all the seasons of life. It's time to reclaim the beauty, power, and blessing of true friendship. Let's begin.

With love,
Marla

The Ten Commandments of Friendship
Acquaintances vs. Friends

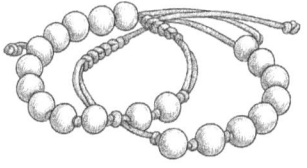

A real friend is someone who would feel loss if you jumped on a train—or in front of one. —Author Unknown

If there's one thing I've learned on my marital journey, as a mom of seven beautiful children, and life coach to women walking through some of life's most challenging seasons, it's this:

Not everyone you meet is your friend. And that's okay.

In today's hyper-connected world, we often confuse access with intimacy. You might know hundreds of people by name, keep up with dozens on social media, and even share laughter and life updates with coworkers, community, or church members; but that doesn't automatically make them your friends.

Friendship, real friendship, is something more profound. It's purposeful. It's intentional. And it's mutual.

What's the Difference?

Sometimes, the line between acquaintance and friend feels blurry, especially when you're a kind, nurturing woman who naturally draws people in. But if you've ever felt hurt or confused when someone didn't show up the way you expected them to, it may be because you mistook an acquaintance for a true friend.

Let's clarify:

An acquaintance is someone you know. You might see them often, work with them, or have casual conversations. But your relationship hasn't reached a level of emotional intimacy, mutual investment, or shared trust.

A friend is someone who walks with you through storms and celebrations. Someone who knows your heart, not just your habits. A friend hears the things you don't say and shows up when you're too weary to ask for help.

Friendship is felt, not just claimed. It's cultivated over time, through trust, and often through trials.

The Danger of Misalignment

One of the most common causes of friendship pain isn't betrayal, it's misalignment. You may call someone your friend while they still see you as a casual connection. You might share your heart with someone who's not prepared to hold it with care. Or, someone might view you as a lifeline while you're simply offering kindness in passing.

Coaching tip: Always pay attention to mutual effort. Friendship is a two-way street. You cannot build a lasting bridge if you're the only one laying bricks.

Before you start trying to fix or deepen a relationship, ask yourself: "Am I the only one carrying the weight of this friendship?" If the answer is yes, be willing to let go and release the guilt, *not the boundary*.

Biblical Wisdom

The Bible reminds us of the beauty, and rarity, of true friendship:

A friend loves at all times, and a brother is born for adversity.
—Proverbs 17:17, NIV

Notice the words "at all times." A friend doesn't disappear when life gets heavy. They love consistently through the wins, losses, and everything in between. Jesus Himself modeled friendship in a profound way when He said:

I have called you friends, for everything that I learned from my Father I have made known to you.
—John 15:15, NIV

True friends share wisdom, truth, and presence. They let you in and walk you through.

Lessons from this chapter:

This chapter was designed to help you:

- Discern who's genuinely in your circle, and who's just passing through.
- Stop giving friendship-level energy to acquaintance-level relationships.
- Love everyone, but invest wisely.
- Embrace the slow, sacred process of building real trust.
- Release unhealthy connections without bitterness or guilt.
- Become a more intentional, discerning, and grace-

filled friend.

Reflection & Coaching Questions

1. Who in your life do you currently call "friend"?
2. Of those individuals, who reciprocates love, effort, and emotional investment?
3. Have you experienced confusion or pain from unmet expectations in a one-sided friendship? If so, what steps have you taken to heal?
4. Are you holding onto a connection that drains more than it blesses? Why?
5. What relationships are worth nurturing more deeply right now, and which ones may need new boundaries?

A Prayer for Clarity and Connection

Heavenly Father,

Thank You for showing me the power of friendship through Your love and example. Help me discern the difference between acquaintances and true friends in my life with wisdom, grace, and peace. Heal any wounds I carry from misaligned relationships, and teach me to love others freely, without losing myself in the process. Surround me with sisters who will walk with me, pray with me, and grow with me. And help me become that kind of friend to others. I trust You to guide my heart and guard my circle.

In Jesus' Name, Amen.

THE TEN COMMANDMENTS OF FRIENDSHIP
40 Qualities of a Good Friend

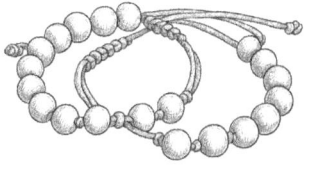

A sweet friendship refreshes the soul.
—Proverbs 27:9, MSG

There are certain people who walk into your life and change everything. Not through grand gestures or loud declarations but simply by being present, consistent, and genuine. These are the friends who refresh your spirit, the ones who show up in the sunshine and in the storm.

As women, we need these kinds of soulful friendships, especially in seasons of building, motherhood, marriage, transitions, and healing. But the truth is, we don't always know how to recognize them.

In a world that often confuses popularity with connection, it's important to step back and ask, *"Who in my life truly brings light into my heart and world, and who dims it?"*

Friendship as a Two-Way Mirror

The 40 qualities in this chapter aren't just about spotting good friends...They're also about becoming one.

A strong friendship doesn't grow from one person doing all the giving. It's a mutual, Spirit-led exchange of love, truth, and trust. So, before you hold others to a standard, gently ask yourself: *Am I showing up this way, too?*

The Ten Commandments Of Friendship

This chapter is your chance to reflect on the friendships you're cultivating, and also to invite God to shape you into the kind of woman others are blessed to walk with.

Biblical Reminder

Two are better than one, because they have a good return for their labor: If either of them falls down, one can help the other up.
—*Ecclesiastes 4:9–10, NIV*

This verse is more than poetic wisdom; it's a truth every woman needs to hold close, especially when life gets hard. God designed us for connection, not competition. He created us to walk alongside each other, not just when everything is going well, but also when things fall apart.

A true friend doesn't just cheer from the sidelines; she steps into your mess, gets her hands dirty, and helps you rise. She notices when your smile is forced, when your joy has faded, when you're too weary to ask for help. And instead of judging or distancing herself, she leans in. She bends low, speaks life into your weary soul, and lifts you with love and prayer.

This kind of friendship is God-given. It's not about surface-level chatter or occasional check-ins. It's about showing up: consistently, compassionately, and without condition. It's about being the kind of woman who says, "You don't have to go through this alone. I'm here. And more importantly, God is, too."

When we live out Ecclesiastes 4:9–10 in our friendships, we become lifelines for each other. We carry one another through the valleys, celebrate on the mountaintops, and reflect the heart of Jesus in how we love, support, and restore each other.

So as you read these pages, ask yourself: Who has lifted

me when I was down? And *who can **I** show up for today, with that same grace-filled strength?* That's the kind of friendship that changes lives.

40 Qualities of a Good Friend

Take this list to heart. Use it to evaluate the people you're closest to. But also? Use it to stretch yourself into becoming the friend your future tribe is praying for, and you will begin to attract what you are.

A good friend is one who:

1. They follow through on what they say.
2. They keep your private matters private.
3. They honor the details of your life with discretion.
4. They respect your time.
5. They check in, not just when they need something.
6. They honor your boundaries, emotional and physical.
7. They have your best interest at heart.
8. They sow positivity into your life.
9. They're givers, not takers.
10. They value your voice and opinions.
11. They uplift and encourage.
12. They believe in your dreams, even when you doubt.
13. They share wisdom and knowledge freely.
14. They show kindness to everyone, not just you.
15. Their presence is helping you grow.
16. Your life is better because they're in it.
17. They support you through seasons and changes.
18. They are committed to growing as a person.
19. They make you feel more courageous.
20. They show up in good times and hard times.

21. They want to spend time with you, and the feeling is mutual.
22. They're kind-hearted and loyal.
23. They increase your confidence and self-worth.
24. Your interactions with them bring joy and peace.
25. They accept you but still speak the truth to help you grow.
26. They give you room to live and evolve.
27. They're honest and trustworthy.
28. You share meaningful interests or purposes.
29. They own up to their mistakes.
30. They speak life over your goals and spirit.
31. Their life inspires you to grow.
32. You feel refreshed after being with them.
33. They offer wise counsel when needed.
34. They protect and look out for you.
35. They help guide you away from destructive paths.
36. You laugh deep belly laughs when you're together.
37. They celebrate your wins with genuine joy.
38. They're present no matter your status or season.
39. Their presence brings peace.
40. You feel truly blessed to know them.

Life Coach Reflection: The Good Friend Check-In

Now that you've read through these 40 qualities, take a few moments to reflect:

1. Which of these traits do your closest friends consistently demonstrate?
2. Which traits do you feel strong in as a friend, and which could use some growth?
3. What relationships in your life need more balance, boundaries, or appreciation?

4. Have you thanked and demonstrated gratitude to your true friends lately for who they are?

Friendship is not about being perfect. It's about being present. Every day is a new opportunity to lean into becoming the kind of friend God designed you to be.

A Prayer to Be and Attract a Good Friend

Dear God,
Thank You for the blessing of friendship. Thank You for the women in my life who have been light in dark places, joy in heavy seasons, and laughter on hard days. Lord, help me recognize those who reflect Your love and truth in my life and release any relationships that are no longer healthy for my heart.

Make me a good friend, Father. Shape my words, my actions, and my presence so I can be someone who uplifts, encourages, and helps others grow. Let me give love generously and receive it humbly. And help me always remember that the friend I want to find, I must also become.

In Jesus' Name, Amen.

THE TEN COMMANDMENTS OF FRIENDSHIP
40 Traits of a Toxic Friend

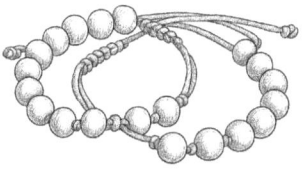

Do not be misled: 'Bad company corrupts good character.'
—1 Corinthians 15:33, NIV

As women, we often pour our hearts into people we believe in; hoping that love, loyalty, or shared history will be enough to sustain the relationship. But sometimes, holding onto the wrong people costs us our peace, our progress, and even our identity.

We've all been there, giving too much, shrinking ourselves, or making excuses for behaviors that drained us. And while grace and forgiveness are holy, so is wisdom.

Let me say this lovingly and clearly: Not every relationship deserves a lifelong seat at your table.

Why This Chapter Matters

As a woman fulfilling many roles and, at times, also experiencing heartbreak, burnout, betrayal, and healing journeys myself while helping other women through theirs, I've seen that one of the most powerful breakthroughs in a woman's life happens when she lets go of a toxic relationship or friendship.

This chapter isn't about judgment. It's about discernment. It's about helping you see clearly so you can protect what God is building in your life. It's about helping you do the brave thing, creating space for healthier, life-giving relationships. Let's walk through this together.

What Is a Toxic Friend?

A toxic friend is someone whose presence consistently brings confusion, chaos, or emotional harm into your life. They may not mean to hurt you, but their patterns repeatedly affect your confidence, clarity, growth, or sense of peace.

Toxicity can manifest as subtle manipulation, bold betrayal, passive-aggressiveness, or emotional abandonment. But no matter the form, the fruit is the same: exhaustion, self-doubt, and a slow erosion of joy.

What Does the Bible Say?

Scripture encourages us to love everyone but also to walk wisely in our relationships.

Walk with the wise and become wise, for a companion of fools suffers harm. —Proverbs 13:20, NIV

And Jesus Himself modeled boundaries. He didn't let everyone close. He was kind to the crowds, but He chose His circle intentionally. It's not un-Christian to walk away from relationships that are damaging to your soul. Sometimes, love means letting go.

40 Toxic Traits to Watch Out For

Use this list to reflect, not just on others but gently on yourself, too. If you see these patterns in your circle or in your own life, it's time to pause, pray, and pivot.

1. They lie repeatedly and without remorse.
2. You feel emotionally drained after being around them.
3. They gossip about your personal business.
4. They rarely support your goals or dreams.
5. They are jealous, possessive, or controlling.
6. They lash out when things don't go their way.
7. They influence you to make poor decisions.
8. They pressure you into things that violate your values.
9. They cross romantic boundaries, disrespecting your past or current relationships.
10. They resent your success or spiritual growth.
11. They take and take but rarely give.
12. They dominate conversations and never ask how you're doing.
13. They only call to dump emotional burdens, never to check in.
14. They contact you just to compare, compete, or one-up.
15. Their advice or influence leads to chaos or regret.
16. They resist your growth or healing journey.
17. The relationship feels one-sided; you're doing all the giving.
18. They only show up when it's convenient.
19. They avoid you or ghost you without explanation.
20. They use sarcasm or silence to punish you.
21. They're only concerned with themselves.
22. They believe gossip before coming to you.
23. They spread lies or rumors behind your back.
24. You feel less confident after interacting with them.
25. They always have to be in control.
26. They monopolize your time or energy.
27. Their competitiveness ruins your connection.

28. They are consistently angry, bitter, or hostile.
29. They blame everyone else and avoid responsibility.
30. They bring dysfunction wherever they go.
31. They ignore or avoid your attempts to connect.
32. They exhibit verbal, emotional, or physical abuse.
33. They show no concern for your emotional well-being.
34. You leave feeling worse, not better.
35. They pull you toward dead-end decisions.
36. They refuse to grow or learn.
37. They disappear unless they need something.
38. They expect generosity but offer little in return.
39. They're unpredictable; you never know what version of them you'll get.
40. You feel like your life was more peaceful before them.

Coaching Insight: Release Without Bitterness

If more than a handful of these traits show up in someone's life, and they're not actively seeking to change, it's okay to step back. The "actively seeking to change" part is critical to being able to move forward in the friendship.

If you see one or two of these traits in yourself, own them gracefully, and begin to actively seek to change yourself. We've all had moments we aren't proud of. Healing starts with honesty.

Don't guilt yourself into staying somewhere God is calling you to leave. Sometimes, the kindest thing you can do is release a friendship so both of you can grow.

Reflection & Coaching Questions:

1. Which of these traits have you experienced in a past

or current friendship?
2. Are there any relationships you've held onto out of obligation instead of alignment?
3. How has this connection impacted your peace, purpose, or progress?
4. What do you need to forgive in yourself or someone else to move forward?
5. Who or what do you need to release so you can make space for authentic sisterhood?

A Prayer for Releasing Toxic Ties

Lord,

Thank You for the clarity to see what is nourishing my spirit, and what is not. Help me release the relationships that no longer reflect the woman You're calling me to be. Give me the courage to set boundaries, the peace to walk away without bitterness, and the wisdom to recognize when it's time to let go.

I trust You to bring the right people into my life, those who will love, uplift, and grow with me in faith. And Lord, help me examine my own heart and heal anything within me that attracts what isn't healthy. I want to love like You do, and also live wisely and well.

In Jesus' Name, Amen.

COMMANDMENT I
Honor Each Other's Boundaries

Real friends respect your no, cheer for your yes, and make space for your growth. —*Marla A. McCarthy*

Above all else, guard your heart, for everything you do flows from it. —*Proverbs 4:23, NIV*

The Friendship Principle: Respect builds trust. Boundaries build lasting friendships.

If you're a woman who wears many hats, you've probably felt the pressure to always be available. As moms, wives, sisters, friends, and businesswomen, we often feel guilty for needing space, saying "no," or not being everything to everyone. But here's the truth. Boundaries aren't barriers; they're bridges to better relationships.

Just like traffic lanes keep drivers safe, emotional and spiritual boundaries keep friendships healthy. As your empowerment and relationship coach, I want to give you permission right now to stop feeling guilty for honoring your needs. More than that, I want you to start expecting the same respect from others that they expect from you.

What Are Boundaries, Really?

The Ten Commandments Of Friendship

Boundaries are spiritual, emotional, physical, and practical guardrails that help you protect what matters most: your peace, your purpose, and your people. Friendship without boundaries leads to burnout, resentment, and emotional exhaustion. But friendship with boundaries? It flourishes in grace, freedom, and longevity.

Let's look at five key areas where boundaries are crucial:

1. Respect Their Time - Time is sacred. It's a gift you can't get back. True friends honor each other's time by showing up when they say they will, being mindful of schedules, and not demanding attention when someone is already stretched thin.

> *Let all things be done decently and in order.*
> *—1 Corinthians 14:40, KJV*

Before texting, venting, or planning a last-minute pop-in, ask, *"Is this a good time?"* A little respect goes a long way.

Coach Tip: Great friends don't compete for time, they protect it.

2. Respect Their Space (aka: the Bubble) - Not everyone is touchy, a hugger, or wants someone in their personal space all the time. Some people recharge with space from others and in quiet. Pay attention to verbal and non-verbal cues. Honor someone's physical and emotional space without taking offense.

Remember: Closeness isn't always about physical proximity; it's about mutual trust and comfort.

3. *Respect Their Other Friendships* - If your friend has more than one close connection, it doesn't mean you're less valuable. In fact, healthy women encourage one another's growth, outside the friendship, too.

Jealousy is a red flag of insecurity. Instead of competing, she should celebrate the circle God has placed around you and your loved ones. There's room for all of us at the table of sisterhood.

A friend loves at all times. —Proverbs 17:17, NIV

4. *Respect Their Relationship with Their Spouse or Partner* - Being a good friend doesn't mean always being first. When your friend is married or in a serious relationship, learn to celebrate their love, even if your life looks different right now.

Never create situations that could tempt, confuse, or pull them away from their commitment. If you truly love your friend, you'll protect their relationship like it's your own.

Coach Tip: A wise friend never pressures their married friend to act single.

5. *Respect Their Resources* - Your friend's time, talents, money, and connections are not owed to you. Gratitude keeps friendships thriving. Entitlement kills them. Be generous, but never manipulative. Share when led, and allow others to do the same without guilt or pressure. You'll be amazed at how your circle becomes more generous when no one feels taken advantage of.

When Boundaries Are Ignored

When someone repeatedly disrespects your boundaries, or when you keep crossing theirs, it chips away at the foundation of trust. If a friend becomes demanding, intrusive, or emotionally manipulative, it's time for an honest conversation.

Boundaries aren't about punishment. They're about protection. They say, "I value this relationship enough to make sure it's sustainable."

If possible, as far as it depends on you, live at peace with everyone. — Romans 12:18, NIV

Empowerment Coaching Reflection:

1. What boundaries do I need to set in my friendships to protect my peace?
2. Am I respecting my friends' time, space, and resources, or expecting too much?
3. Have I been afraid to speak up because I don't want to hurt someone's feelings?
4. How would my relationships change if I led with grace and clarity?

Friendship Coaching Questions:

1. What are your personal boundaries, and are you clearly communicating them?
2. What boundaries have you noticed your friends value (even if they haven't said them)?
3. Are there any relationships where you feel your boundaries are being crossed?
4. Who do you need to have a gentle conversation with this week?
5. What kind of friend do you want to be known as

when it comes to honoring boundaries?

A Prayer for Friendship Boundaries

Father God,

Thank You for teaching me that boundaries are not a burden, they are a blessing. Help me to love others without losing myself. Show me how to honor the time, space, and hearts of those I call friends. Give me courage to speak with grace and humility when I feel overwhelmed or unheard. May my friendships reflect Your order, Your peace, and Your unconditional love.

In Jesus' Name, Amen.

Sisterhood Reminder:

You matter, and so do your boundaries. Healthy friendship isn't about saying *yes* to everything. It's about knowing when to say *no* with love and trusting that a true sister will honor that 'no'.

Remember, boundaries aren't walls that push people away; they're gates that protect what's sacred: your peace, your time, your healing, your wholeness.

When we respect each other's boundaries, we give our friendships room to breathe. We allow space for grace to flow, for wounds to heal, and for trust to deepen. Real sisterhood isn't built on pressure, guilt, or overextension; it's built on mutual respect, open communication, and God-centered love.

If you want friendships that last through life's changing seasons: of building, motherhood, marriage, heartbreak, career shifts, caregiving, and grief. Build them on honor, not obligation. Give each other the freedom to rest, to reset, and to grow. That's when friendship becomes a safe place, not another source of stress.

So let this be your reminder: you are allowed to take up space. You are allowed to protect your energy. And any friendship rooted in God's Word will not only survive your boundaries; it will thrive because of them.

Commandment II
Celebrate Her Wins Like They're Your Own

Rejoice with those who rejoice; mourn with those who mourn.
—Romans 12:15, NIV

The Friendship Principle:

A real sister-friend claps when you win, loudly, joyfully, and without envy.

This world has enough critics and competitors. What does it need more of? Cheerleaders. Celebrators. Confetti-throwing sisters who know how to uplift one another.

It's easy to feel excited when it's your turn, when the spotlight is on you, or when God is answering your prayers. But what about when it's someone else's moment? Do you show up then, too?

As your coach, I want you to know that how you respond to your friends' victories reveals the health of your own heart. If you've ever caught yourself feeling insecure, overlooked, or a little "less than" while someone else shines, breathe beautiful. You're not alone. Let's walk through this together.

Her Win Is Not Your Loss

Sometimes it stings a little when someone else gets the

thing you've been praying for. The engagement. The promotion. The baby. The house. The breakthrough. You want to celebrate, but deep down you wonder, *"God... what about me?"*

Here's the truth your heart needs to hear today: When God blesses another woman, it's not a rejection of you; *it's a reminder.* A reminder that He's still moving. That He's still writing stories. That your chapter isn't finished yet.

We are not in competition; we are in community. God's kingdom doesn't operate on scarcity; it runs on abundance. That means there is room at the table for all of us. Her success doesn't diminish your value. Her joy doesn't erase your story. In fact, her win may be the encouragement your faith needs right now. Because if God did it for her, He can do it for you too: in His time, in His way, and for your good.

That's why it's so powerful when women stop comparing and start cheering each other on. When we rise together, we reflect the heart of heaven. We become a sisterhood that claps when others shine, even if we're still waiting for our own spotlight because we trust, deep in our souls, that what God has for me is for me.

This isn't just a catchy phrase. It's a truth whispered by generations of praying women who have seen God come through, time and time again. Women who have learned to celebrate others while standing in faith for their own breakthrough.

So the next time you see her win, let your soul smile. Let it strengthen your belief. Because her blessing is not a threat; it's a preview. And if God is handing out miracles in your neighborhood, you can be sure He hasn't forgotten your address.

What Should We Celebrate?

Friendships are watered by intentional celebration. Here are just a few life moments that deserve your applause:

- Birthdays & anniversaries
- Promotions or new businesses
- Engagements, marriages, and adoptions
- Personal growth, milestones, and spiritual breakthroughs
- Recoveries, healing, and testimonies
- Answered prayers, big or small
- When she finally leaves the toxic job, the toxic man, or the toxic mindset
- When she finally finds the one who lifts her up, encourages her dreams, and feeds her soul

Every one of these is a "praise break" opportunity in your friendship.

Coaching Moment: Why It's Hard Sometimes

If you've ever felt a twinge of jealousy or sadness when someone else receives something you're still waiting on, pause and extend yourself grace.

Then ask:

1. What does this moment reveal about what I believe is possible for me?
2. Am I secretly afraid that my turn won't come?
3. Do I need to refocus on my goals so I can celebrate hers with a full heart?

Your emotions aren't the problem. But what you do with them matters.

Action Breaks Fear

Fear says: "Her win means less for me." Faith says: "God is still writing my story, and it's going to be good." So next time you feel that twist in your chest? Pray, plan, and then clap anyway. Celebrate her, not just because she deserves it; but because you do too, in order to be free from comparison.

How to Celebrate Your Friend (With or Without Spending a Dime)

Celebration is more than balloons, brunches, or boutique gifts; it's a *spiritual posture*. It's saying with your words and actions, *"I see you. I honor your growth. I'm cheering you on."* You don't need a big budget to make a big impact. What your friend needs most isn't something expensive; it's something authentic.

Your *presence* will always mean more than your *presents*. Why? Because genuine celebration reminds a woman that she matters not just for what she has accomplished, but simply for who she is.

Here are a few heartfelt and powerful ways to show up for your sister-friend, no price tag required:

- Send a voice note saying, "I'm proud of you," or "I see the woman you're becoming."
- Shout her out on social media, not just for the world to see, but to affirm her purpose, growth, or strength.
- Mail a handwritten card or send a thoughtful text with a simple but soul-touching message like, "You inspire me more than you know."
- Host a potluck or game night just to honor her.

Make it fun, personal, and filled with laughter.
- Create something with your hands or heart: a poem, a playlist, a baked good, a craft. Yes, you are creative, and your effort means everything.

Coach Tip: The most meaningful celebrations reflect her love language, not just yours. If she values words, speak them. If she treasures time, offer it. Celebration is about intentional love, not grand gestures.

When we celebrate each other well, we remind the world what real sisterhood looks like: joyful, generous, and rooted in love. So go ahead, honor her. Lift her. And in doing so, become the kind of friend every woman silently hopes for.

Empowerment Reflection Questions:

1. Who in your life needs to hear "I'm proud of you" today?
2. What holds you back from celebrating others freely?
3. How can you create a lifestyle of celebration: one that's joyful, generous, and judgment-free?

Friendship Coaching Practice:

1. Make a list of your close friends.
2. Add their key dates (birthdays, anniversaries, etc.) to your calendar.
3. Choose one way you'll intentionally celebrate each friend this season, big or small.
4. Text or call someone today with sincere congratulations about a recent win.

Prayer: A Heart That Celebrates

Dear God,

Thank You for reminding me that there is no shortage of blessings in Your Kingdom. Help me to celebrate my sisters with genuine love and joy. Remove envy, fear, and comparison from my heart. Fill me with gratitude, expectancy, and compassion. I declare that I am not in competition with anyone. I am becoming better daily *for me* and to fulfill my purpose and destiny. I am rooted in love, walking in purpose, and cheering loudly for every woman rising into her divine destiny.

In Jesus' Name, Amen.

Final Encouragement

Friendship is a gift from God. It's not just a social connection; it's a sacred assignment. When we choose to truly celebrate one another instead of merely tolerating each other, we create a space where joy doesn't just visit; it takes root. In that space, confidence blossoms, purpose is affirmed, and God's love flows freely.

This kind of sisterhood is rare, but it's possible. It starts with us choosing to show up with open hearts, kind words, lifted hands, and yes, even confetti and balloons when needed. It means praying for your friend's miracle while believing God hasn't forgotten yours. It means clapping with your whole heart, even if you're still in the waiting room of your own breakthrough.

Let's be the kind of women who don't withhold celebration out of insecurity or comparison, but who give it freely because we know there's more than enough goodness to go around. Your time is coming, too. And when it does, you'll look around and see that the very women you celebrated…

are now the ones celebrating you.

This is the power of friendship and sisterhood. Let's protect it. Let's cherish it. And most of all, let's live it, with bold love, deep faith, and joyful hearts.

Commandment III
Protect Her Kindness, Don't Take Advantage

The only way to have a friend is to be one.
—Ralph Waldo Emerson

Do to others as you would have them do to you.
—Luke 6:31, NIV

Let's talk about kindness. Not the hashtag or the cute coffee mug quote, but the real-life, sacrificial, behind-the-scenes kind of kindness.

The kind that costs someone time, energy, and emotional labor. The kind that makes someone pause their own chaos to lean into yours. The kind that is freely given, but should never be taken for granted.

As women, wives, moms, sisters, and friends, we pour out so much. And when someone chooses to pour back into you with grace, gifts, support, or time, it is sacred. It's a blessing. And it should never be exploited.

True Kindness Is a Gift

Some people hand out kindness like confetti. Others guard it closely, offering it only after trust is earned. Either way, when someone chooses to be kind to you, recognize it as a gift.

In today's culture, kindness often gets mistaken for weakness. But let me tell you something: there is nothing weak about a woman who chooses to give generously while expecting nothing in return. That's strength. That's love. That's friendship.

Kindness is loaning someone your strength instead of reminding them of their weakness. — Andy Stanley

What Exploiting Kindness Looks Like

Sometimes, we don't even realize we've crossed a line. But here are a few ways to check yourself:

1. *Tangible Generosity* - When a friend brings you food, loans you money, or buys you a gift, you begin to expect it, even demand it. Kindness is not an entitlement. It's a choice.

Empowerment Tip: When someone gives, pause and say, Thank you. You didn't have to do that, but you did. And I don't take it for granted."

2. *Acts of Service* - She babysits your kids, runs errands, and helps with your project, but you stop saying thank you. You assume she'll always be there.

Empowerment Tip: The next time someone helps you, ask yourself: Have I been as giving to her as she's been to me?

3. *Her Time* - This is the big one. Time is the most valuable thing we have, and once it's gone, it's gone forever.

Empowerment Tip: Before you call, text, or pop over, ask: Is this a good time? Honor her schedule, her time, her energy, and her season.

Coaching Check-In: Motives Matter

Let's pause for a heart check. Sometimes we do the right thing, but with the wrong heart. Perhaps you brought her a meal, supported her business, or helped her through a difficult time. But deep down, was your kindness freely given… or secretly tied to an unspoken expectation?

Here's the hard truth: If your actions are rooted in the hope of control, praise, or payback, they're not acts of love; they're transactions. And true friendship isn't a business deal. It's a gift.

God calls us to serve one another out of genuine love, not quiet manipulation. Not guilt. Not obligation. When we give from a place of purity, there's freedom for you and for her. But when our help comes with hidden strings, we not only poison the relationship, we exhaust ourselves emotionally.

So take a deep breath and ask yourself:

- Did I give to bless her heart, or to secure her loyalty?
- Am I punishing her through distance, silence, or resentment because she didn't respond the way I wanted?
- Can I release this with grace and trust God to see my heart, even if she didn't?

Healthy friendships are built on grace, not scorekeeping. You don't need to earn love, and neither does she.

When you release the need for reciprocation, your love becomes powerful, healing, and free.

Remember: The motive matters as much as the moment. And your heart deserves to be at peace with how you show up.

The Emotional Debt Trap

Let's talk about a trap too many women fall into: emotional debt. Just because someone once helped you, supported you, or showed you kindness, doesn't mean you now owe them your entire life. And the same goes the other way, you don't get to collect on love like it's a bill waiting to be paid.

Gratitude is a beautiful response. But it's just that, a response. Not a contract. Healthy friendship is rooted in mutual respect and freedom, not guilt or silent obligation. Love doesn't demand repayment; it invites honor.

So, how do we honor love without falling into emotional debt? We acknowledge the gift. We express sincere appreciation. And most importantly, we never weaponize the past. Because once love is used as leverage, it ceases to be love. It becomes control.

Here's what that might sound like in your spirit-check:

- "I'm not required to overextend myself to prove I'm thankful."
- "I can appreciate her generosity without feeling obligated to say yes to everything."
- "I'm allowed to grow and create boundaries, even if she once helped me through a hard time."

Likewise, if you've ever said, "After all I've done for her..." as a way to justify resentment, pause and reflect; true generosity releases expectations. It doesn't keep score.

And remember this wisdom:

Before borrowing money from a friend, decide which you need most.
—American Proverb

Sometimes the real cost isn't financial; it's relational. Friendship isn't about debt. It's about dignity. And when we let go of emotional IOUs, we create space for love to flow freely, without guilt, without manipulation, and without hidden terms.

Empowerment Reflection Questions:

1. Have I taken anyone's kindness for granted?
2. Who in my life has been generous with their time, gifts, or energy, and needs to hear a heartfelt thank you?
3. Do I give with a pure heart, or do I silently keep score?
4. Am I crowding someone's emotional space and calling it friendship?

Coaching Assignment:

Make a gratitude list: Write down at least three people who have shown you kindness lately. Send each of them a thank-you text, card, or call this week.

Set a kindness goal: Who can you bless this week with your time, gifts, or encouragement without expecting anything in return?

The Ten Commandments Of Friendship

Prayer: A Heart That Gives Freely & Gratefully

Heavenly Father,

Thank You for the gift of kindness. Teach me to recognize it, honor it, and never take it for granted. Help me to give freely and receive humbly. Show me how to be a friend who sows love, not manipulation; gratitude, not guilt. Let me be a reflection of Your heart in every friendship.

In Jesus' Name, Amen.

Final Thought

Kindness is currency in the kingdom of God and in friendship. Give it generously. Receive it gratefully. Protect it fiercely.

Always remember: People don't leave because you weren't perfect, they leave because they didn't feel valued. So, let's value one another deeply and build the kind of friendships that heal, not hurt.

Commandment IV
Speak the Truth in Love

A friend accepts us as we are yet helps us to be what we should.
—*Author Unknown*

Wounds from a friend can be trusted, but an enemy multiplies kisses. —*Proverbs 27:6, NIV*

We all want real. Real love. Real connection. Real friends who show up and speak up. But here's the truth: *Real* takes courage.

One of the most loving things you can do for a friend is tell her the truth with gentleness, grace, and a heart full of love. That's what real sisterhood is built on, not silent resentment or fake smiles but open communication and honesty that heals instead of harms.

Truth Telling Is an Act of Love

Being truthful doesn't mean being harsh. It means you value your friend enough to be honest, even when it's hard. And you do it in a way that honors who she is, what she's going through, and with the grace you hope to receive in return.

The Ten Commandments Of Friendship

"A friend is someone who knows the song in your heart and can sing it back to you when you've forgotten the words."
—*C.S. Lewis (adapted)*

When a friend is going off course, hurting others (or herself), or doing something that jeopardizes your relationship, silence is not loyalty. Truth, *spoken in love*, is.

Why We Don't Speak Up

Too often, we stay quiet because we're afraid:

- Afraid of conflict.
- Afraid of ruining the friendship.
- Afraid of being misunderstood or pushed away.

But holding in your truth builds resentment, and resentment poisons closeness. It's better to say something gently now than let unspoken issues grow into full-blown bitterness later. Silence may keep the peace today, but honesty protects the friendship for tomorrow.

How to Tell the Truth with Love

Before you speak:

1. Pray. Ask God to give you the right words and the right heart.
2. Prepare. Think about what you want to say and why.
3. Pause. Consider her feelings, her season, and your tone.

Then, speak:

- Privately. Don't embarrass her; pull her aside.
- Lovingly. Start with affirmations. Remind her of how much you care.
- Clearly. Don't beat around the bush; get to the heart of the matter.
- Gently. Use "I feel" or "I've noticed" instead of attacking.
- Humbly. Stay open to hearing the truth about yourself, too.

And When You're on the Receiving End…

Remember: Truth hurts… but it heals. When someone you love brings truth to you (hard, uncomfortable, soul-stretching truth), pause before you react. Don't shut down. Don't snap back. Don't disappear. Pause. Breathe. Reflect.

Ask yourself honestly: *"Is there any truth in what she's saying, even if it's hard to hear?"*

True friends are not just hype women; they're heart women. They love you too much to let you stay stuck in unhealthy patterns, blind spots, or small thinking. They'll gently, or sometimes boldly, hold up a mirror, not to shame you, but to help you see.

And yes, truth can sting. But it's a sting that saves.

A real sister won't always tell you what you want to hear. She'll tell you what you need to hear because she wants to see you rise, not just remain. That kind of honesty is a divine gift. Receive it with humility. Sit with it. Pray over it. And if needed, grow from it.

Because at the end of the day, growth and comfort rarely live in the same space.

Remember the wise words of Frances Ward Weller:

The Ten Commandments Of Friendship

"A friend can tell you things you don't want to tell yourself."

Honor the friend who loves you enough to tell you the truth. That's not betrayal; that's bravery. And it's one of the purest forms of love you'll ever receive.

When Truth Goes Unspoken

Have you ever let something small slide… only to realize it's quietly growing roots in your heart? Maybe it was a comment that rubbed you the wrong way. A moment when you felt overlooked. A promise that went unfulfilled. You didn't say anything at the time, maybe because you didn't want to cause tension, or perhaps because you weren't sure how to put your feelings into words.

So you smiled. You nodded. You kept showing up.

But inside? You started to pull away. The calls slowed. The texts grew shorter. And now, there's distance she doesn't even understand.

Sis, that's not peace; *it's avoidance.* And while avoidance feels safer in the moment, it slowly erodes the very trust that makes friendship sacred. Real sisterhood isn't built on surface-level smiles or swept-under-the-rug offenses. It's built on brave conversations. Healing honesty. Loving truth.

God never meant for us to live behind masks of politeness or perform our way through relationships. Scripture calls us to something deeper:

Instead, speaking the truth in love, we will grow to become in every respect the mature body of him who is the head, that is, Christ.
—Ephesians 4:15, NIV

Spiritual maturity isn't just about knowing Scripture; it's about living it. And that means learning to speak up before bitterness takes root.

True friends don't avoid; they engage. Not to criticize, but to clear the air. Not to control, but to restore connection. Because when truth is spoken in love, hearts heal, trust deepens, and the friendship becomes stronger than before.

Don't let silence steal what God meant to grow. Be brave. Be honest. Be loving. That's what real sisterhood looks like.

Coaching Insight: The Pie Isn't About the Pie

The Strawberry Pie Incident

Let's discuss a story about a family. For months, this family was frustrated and fractured. One particular family member had thrown a full-blown tantrum, yet no one was willing to address it. The silent treatment towards a family member was dished out, and the tension lingered, and emotional damage was done. Eventually, after time passed and emotions cooled, they learned the root of the problem, and it was downright silly.

The family member dishing out the silent treatment claimed her feelings were hurt, over a pie. Yes, you read that right, a strawberry pie. This fully capable, physically healthy individual allowed her pride, possible jealously, and selfishness to cloud her judgment to the point where she nearly broke the family, over a pie. She ignored and withheld affection from a family member who, truth be told, was already going through serious health challenges. And it was all over a strawberry pie recipe.

Now, we know enough about human behavior to realize it probably wasn't just about the pie or about the recipe at all. That pie was just the surface-level trigger. But the lesson here is essential: how often do we allow petty, unresolved issues to fester and create distance in our relationships? All because we're too prideful, or too afraid, to be honest about what we are feeling and why. And to say what we really feel.

So, in honor of what is now lovingly referred to as *The Strawberry Pie Incident*, let this be your gentle nudge to self-reflect. If you're currently upset with someone, especially for something that, in hindsight, might be minor, press pause on reading this book and go reach out and talk to them. Reconnect. Be the grown-up. Be the bigger person.

Loss of life has taught me that life is far too short to let something small drive a permanent wedge between you and someone you love. The worst regret is the one you feel when someone leaves this earth and you never took the chance to make things right.

If there is someone you need to make it right with, pause right now from reading this book and take a step, make a phone call, or send a text.

Sis, we're living without regrets the best we can from this point forward. If you felt even a little nudge right now reading this about anything or anyone, pray about it and make a move.

If you struggle to say the words out loud, write them in a letter. Be honest. Be kind. Then, give them the space to respond in their own way and in their own time. Whether they reply how you hoped or not isn't the point. What matters most is that you choose healing over holding a grudge. Because at the end of the day, you can only control one person, yourself.

Sometimes we explode over something that seems small, like a pie. But it's not about the pie. It's about what the pie represents: being overlooked, being hurt, feeling unseen or not good enough ourselves. Sometimes, our reaction is because of hurt, betrayal, or rejection that happened previously in our lives and has nothing to do with the person we are currently in a relationship with.

When we don't speak up, we start interpreting every action through the lens of our pain. That's why it's so essential to check in about what we are really feeling and why and to speak up sooner rather than later in our friendships. Say what's on your heart while there's still time to heal the relationship or repair the connection.

Truth Builds Trust

Friendship without honesty is like a house without a foundation. One strong storm, and everything falls apart. Truth may feel risky, but it's also what keeps relationships honest and real. It builds trust, depth, and intimacy.

So, when something's bothering you, don't let it sit. Don't let it simmer. And definitely don't let it turn into gossip. Go directly to your friend. Pray for grace. Speak from the heart. Then, listen.

Reflection Questions:

1. Who have I not been honest with because I've been afraid of their reaction?
2. What truth have I been holding back that needs to be said with love?
3. How would I want someone to tell me something difficult?
4. What truth do I need to hear, but have been avoiding?
5. Am I a safe place for my friends to be honest?

Prayer for Bold & Loving Honesty

Dear Lord,

Help me to be the kind of friend who speaks truth with grace. Let my words build up, not tear down. Give me the wisdom to know when to speak, the courage to do it, and the compassion to do it in love. Help me to be a safe place for others to grow, and give me the strength to hear the truth about myself, too.

In Jesus' Name, Amen.

Real Talk Recap

Truth spoken in love is one of the greatest gifts you can give and receive in friendship. If something's wrong, *say it*. But say it gently. Make honesty your habit and love your anchor. Don't lose a friendship over something that could've been healed with one honest conversation. Truth doesn't end friendships, silence does. And the friendships that are meant to last will only grow stronger when rooted in truth.

COMMANDMENT V
Practice Compassion Over Criticism

To have a good friend is one of the highest delights of life; to be a good friend is one of the noblest and most difficult undertakings.
—Anonymous

Rejoice with those who rejoice; mourn with those who mourn.
—Romans 12:15, NIV

The Heart of Friendship Is Empathy

At its deepest level, friendship isn't about being the funniest, the busiest, or the one who always has the right answer. It's not about being constantly available *or* showing up only when it's fun, convenient, or Instagram-worthy.

True friendship is *love in motion.* It's presence with purpose.

At the heart of it all is **empathy,** the special space where love and understanding intersect. It's that moment when you set aside your own agenda to truly see your friend, not just her highlight reel, but her hidden pain, her silent battles, and her everyday courage.

Empathy says:

- "I may not fully understand, but I'm here to listen."

- "I won't rush you. I'll sit with you."
- "I choose to feel with you, not fix you."

It's choosing compassion over criticism, patience over pressure, and connection over convenience. It's remembering that sometimes the most powerful ministry you can offer isn't advice; it's simply your presence.

When you transition from reaction to reverence, from opinion to understanding, your friendships undergo a profound transformation. They deepen. They become safe places where both joy and sorrow can breathe without judgment.

Empathy is the heartbeat of every soul-deep sisterhood. When we love with empathy, we reflect the very heart of Jesus, who didn't just tell people He loved them; He demonstrated it through His actions. He entered into their pain and remained.

So, slow down. Look up. Lean in. Someone in your life may not need a solution; they just need a soft place to land. Be that place.

Selfishness Is the Silent Killer

Most of us have had seasons where we were more self-focused than we'd like to admit. But here's a gentle nudge: If you never ask your friends how they're doing, if you dominate every conversation, or if you only reach out when you need something, this chapter is for you, sis.

Here are a few signs that self-centeredness may be sabotaging your friendships:

- You constantly vent but rarely listen.
- You call friends only when you're in crisis but disappear when they need support.

- You can't recall the last time you asked how someone else was really doing.
- You struggle to remember important events or updates in their life.

If any of these hit home, *breathe,* acknowledge the need to change but release the guilt, and give yourself grace. Growth begins with *awareness.* Now is a beautiful time to course-correct and become the kind of friend your heart desires.

What Is Empathy?

Empathy is not just "feeling bad" for someone. It's a deep, heart-led understanding of what someone is going through, even if their life looks different from yours.

It's:
1. Asking how someone's doing and *actually listening.*
2. Being present without trying to fix everything.
3. Remembering important details that matter to them.
4. Considering their perspective before making assumptions.

Putting Yourself in Her Shoes

The most transformational friendships are rooted in empathy. Empathy starts by pausing one's own internal dialogue long enough to be present for someone else.

Be completely humble and gentle; be patient, bearing with one another in love. —Ephesians 4:2, NIV

Friendship isn't always about showing up with a solution, it's often about showing up period.

Real-life Coaching Insight

Let's say your friend didn't text you back right away. Instead of assuming she's ignoring you, ask: "Could she be overwhelmed? Tired? Dealing with something I don't know about?"

Empathy allows you to interpret situations through a lens of love instead of insecurity. It makes you a safe space, and trust me, women remember who made them feel safe *and seen,* even on their worst days.

When You Can't Be There…

There will be seasons when you're the one going through it: your plate is full, your schedule is stretched, and your heart feels heavy. In those moments, a true friend will offer you the same empathy and grace you've shown them.

If you're not able to support someone in the way they want, be honest. Let them know they're still deeply loved. You're just temporarily overwhelmed. Real friends don't keep score; they understand that life has seasons.

"The Golden Rule" isn't just a quote, it's a guide for growing godly friendships.

Shift from Me-Focused to We-Focused

Empathy doesn't require money or grand gestures. Sometimes, all it takes is:

- A text that says, *"Thinking of you today"*
- A prayer whispered for her breakthrough

- A five-minute call just to listen
- A reminder that she's not alone in what she's going through

You may not be able to fix her problem, but your love can be the soft place she lands when life feels hard.

Empathy Is the Gift That Keeps Giving

So then, in everything treat others the same way you want them to treat you… —Matthew 7:12, AMP

When you give empathy, you create emotional safety. And where there is emotional safety, there is vulnerability, growth, joy, and true friendship.

This doesn't mean you neglect your own needs or abandon your goals. It simply means you expand your capacity to love *beyond your own comfort.* And the beautiful thing? You become a woman who is deeply loved and richly trusted in return.

Reflection Questions

1. Who in your life needs your empathy right now?
2. When was the last time you asked someone how they were doing, and really listened?
3. Have you been showing up only when you need something, or have you also sown into others?
4. Are there friends who may be feeling unseen by you? If so, how can you change that starting today?
5. What would it look like to show love that asks nothing in return?

The Ten Commandments Of Friendship

A Prayer for an Empathetic Heart

Dear God,

Give me a heart that mirrors Yours: gentle, kind, and full of compassion. Help me to see beyond my own needs and extend love where it's needed most. Show me how to show up for my sisters, not with perfection, but with presence. Let me be the kind of friend I would want for myself, one who listens, loves, and lifts. And when I fall short, help me to try again with grace.

In Jesus' Name, Amen.

Real Talk Recap

Empathy is love in action. It asks "How are you?" and *truly cares about the answer.* Avoid being the friend who only shows up when she needs something. Practice patience, compassion, and presence, even when life is busy. Empathy makes space for others while trusting that what's for you will still find you. You don't lose anything by loving well, only selfishness loses when empathy wins.

Commandment VI
Let Go of Control and Let Her Be Herself

A true friend never gets in your way unless you happen to be going down. —Arnold H. Glasow

It is for freedom that Christ has set us free.
—Galatians 5:1, NIV

Real Friendship Leaves Room to Breathe

Friendship is not ownership. It's not about manipulation, control, or demanding someone live life according to your timeline, preferences, or expectations. Real friendship gives space. Real love gives *freedom*.

Controlling behavior is often rooted in fear: fear of being left behind, of losing someone, of not getting what you want. But friend, fear cannot be the foundation of any relationship meant to thrive.

Let go, trust God, and let your friend be her full, free, God-designed self.

What Control Really Looks Like

Control can wear a lot of disguises:

- Guilt trips

- Silent treatment
- Micromanaging her time
- Manipulating her with past favors
- Overstepping boundaries
- Moodiness when things don't go your way

If you've ever thought:

- "Why didn't she invite me?"
- "She didn't text back fast enough."
- "She's too close with that new friend."

Take a pause. Take a breath. Ask yourself: Is this about her, *or is this about something unresolved in me?* Is this about me not being focused and productive in my own life? Is this really about me not working on my own goals or living out my life purpose?

Heart Check: What Are You Really Afraid Of?

Every controlling tendency has a root. Ask yourself:

1. What am I afraid of losing?
2. Why do I feel the need to manage someone else's choices?
3. What part of my life feels out of control right now?
4. What could I be building instead of trying to control someone else?
5. What would I be free to do if I stopped obsessing over this?

Sis, this is not judgment. This is your moment of empowered reflection. God is not calling you to control people. He's calling you to control your thoughts, emotions, actions, and focus. He's calling you to focus so you can fulfill *your* purpose.

You Are the Steward of Your Life, Not Hers

Many are the plans in a person's heart, but it is the Lord's purpose that prevails. —Proverbs 19:21, NIV

As women who care deeply, it's easy to want the best for the people we love. We want to protect them from poor choices, encourage them to reach their potential, and intervene when we see them drifting. But here's a gentle reminder, sis: *you are not responsible for someone else's journey.*

You're not her Holy Spirit. You're not her life coach unless she hired you. And even then, your role is to support, not control.

You are her friend. Her encourager. Her prayer partner. Her safe space. Not her manager, fixer, or decision-maker.

Even when you can clearly see a better path, it's not your job to take the pen from God's hand and try to rewrite her story. She has her own journey, just like you do, and God is leading her through it, even if the pace *or process* looks different from yours.

Focus on stewarding your own calling so well that you don't have time to micromanage hers. Be present, be prayerful, be patient. And when needed, offer wisdom with grace, not control.

Because true friendship releases, it doesn't restrain. It trusts God's timing, even when you don't understand it. And it honors the sacred space between two women who are each becoming who God created them to be, at their own pace, in their own way, under His guidance.

When You're the One Being Controlled

Let's shift the perspective for a moment. If you've been feeling unheard, manipulated, or emotionally weighed down in a friendship, this is for you.

Perhaps you're always the one adjusting, apologizing, explaining, and overextending just to keep the peace. Maybe you've been questioning your own voice, your worth, your right to say *"enough."*

Here's the loving truth: You are not here to be managed. Your life belongs to God, not to your friends, not to their opinions, not to their expectations.

And yes, your voice matters. Your boundaries matter. Your peace matters.

You have every right to:

- Set healthy limits.
- Say "no" without guilt, apology, or over-explaining.
- Prioritize your peace over people-pleasing.
- Walk away from friendships that suffocate instead of support.
- Create space for God to heal what manipulation tried to silence.

Jesus Himself said:

Let your yes be yes and your no, no. —Matthew 5:37, NKJV

That means you're allowed to be clear. You're allowed to stand firm. And you're allowed to protect the space God is growing you in, without shame.

A healthy friendship never demands your silence, submission, or your soul. It honors your boundaries. It listens when you speak. It grows with you. And if it doesn't? You are allowed to *let go in love* and trust that God will surround you with the kind of sisterhood that sees, values, and uplifts you.

You don't have to shrink to keep anyone. You were never meant to live small just to make others comfortable. You were meant to live free.

Give Her Room to Grow: Without Resentment

You don't need to be involved in every detail of your friend's life to still be important in it. Sometimes, she needs space to:

- Focus on her mental health.
- Navigate motherhood or marriage.
- Heal from hurt.
- Chase a goal or dream God whispered only to her.

Giving your friend space isn't rejection, it's respect. It's respect for who she is and the plans and purposes for which she was created. It's respecting that she deserves room to grow. A garden only grows and thrives when each plant has enough room to stretch toward the sun.

Coaching Insight: Stop Being the Main Character in Her Story

We all love to feel needed. But friendships don't thrive when you're trying to be the sun, moon, and stars in someone else's life.

Here's what real friendship sounds like:
- *"I'm here when you need me."*

- *"I support your decision even if I don't fully understand."*
- *"You have the right to take space, grow, and be who God created you to be."*

That's what maturity and love look like. And those friendships last.

Real Talk Reflection

1. Who are you trying to manage or change, rather than simply love?
2. Is there anyone you need to release to God: a friend, sibling, spouse, child? (*Life and sanity tip:* Allow them to be on God's Potter's Wheel...and take your hands out of the clay.)
3. What will happen if you just pray, release it to God, and stop trying to control the outcome?
4. What would happen if you focused all that energy on your own healing, growth, and purpose?
5. Who in your life do you need to set clear boundaries with?

A Prayer for Release of Control:

Dear Lord,

Thank You for the blessing of sisterhood; the kind of friendship that fills our lives with joy, encouragement, and growth. Today, I surrender the need to control what I was never created to carry. Help me, God, to let go of my expectations, timelines, and silent or loud demands I've placed on others, especially the women I love.

Give me the grace to love her freely, to celebrate her growth, even when it's apart from me. Teach me to trust You with her journey just as I trust You with mine. If there's insecurity in me, heal it. If there's fear, calm it. If there's pride, soften it. Remind me that I am called to be a friend, not a fixer. A supporter, not a supervisor. A safe space, not a stumbling block.

And when I'm the one being controlled, give me strength to set healthy boundaries and protect the peace You've called me to walk in. Thank You, Lord, for being in control so I don't have to be.

I release the weight. I receive Your peace. And I trust You with the friendship. Whatever comes, whatever happens, I know You've got me.

In Jesus' Name, Amen.

Final Reminder:

Friendship is a garden, not a cage. Give her space. Give her grace. Give yourself permission to focus on your own lane, your own plot of land, territory, and purpose, and watch both of you bloom.

The most beautiful discovery true friends make is that they can grow separately without growing apart.
—Elisabeth Foley

The Ten Commandments Of Friendship

COMMANDMENT VII
Show Up When It Matters Most

If a friend is in trouble, don't annoy them by asking if there's anything you can do. Think up something appropriate—and do it. —Edgar Watson Howe

Carry each other's burdens, and in this way you will fulfill the law of Christ. —Galatians 6:2, NIV

Real Friends Don't Just Talk, They Show Up

Let's be real. Life gets heavy sometimes. And just like buildings need beams to stand tall and bridges need cables to hold weight, people need support to get through life's storms.

That's what friendship is supposed to be: A soft place to land, a hand to hold. A voice that says, "I got you."

I've been through many challenging seasons. When my husband had multiple strokes, many friends and family showed up in an "I've got you" kind of way. One particular couple we've known for years, I promise, it felt like they came bursting through the front door with support and groceries for the kids before the last sentence of what had happened to my husband had been shared with everyone.

When I was emotionally stable enough to joke about it later, the husband of that couple said to me that sometimes you don't need to ask what you can do, *just do something*.

That's precisely what they did. That was so helpful because my mind was so scattered when it initially occurred that it was hard for me to assess what the needs of my family were. But the kindness of the people in our lives ensured that I could be at the hospital and that my children would be taken care of, fed, and be able to continue in their school and extra-curricular activity schedules as normal as possible under those circumstances.

I could not be more grateful for all the people who listened to God's voice, became God's hands and feet on the earth, and moved to support us when that tragic moment happened in our lives. God showed me through them that He's got us, always has, always will. There are no words to fully express my gratitude.

So, let's talk about what it means *for you* to actually show up.

First, Know Your Limits

Support doesn't mean martyrdom. You don't have to lose yourself to be there for someone else. You can't give what you don't have. Giving from a place of guilt or pressure instead of love and a cheerful heart only creates resentment.

So, check your heart:

- Can I give this freely and joyfully?
- Will I regret doing this later?
- Am I trying to be the savior… or a sister?

Healthy support has boundaries. And when your support is rooted in love, not obligation, it becomes life-giving for both of you.

The Power of Presence

Sometimes, the most powerful thing you can give someone is your presence. Not advice. Not solutions. Not a long list of "what they should've done differently." *Just. Be. There.* Be the friend who shows up when no one else does. The one who says, "You don't have to go through this alone. Even if it's just sitting quietly in the room, sending a voice note, or praying behind the scenes, your presence is a gift.

Be Thoughtful with Your Time

Life is extremely full, no question about it. Between work, motherhood, marriage, caregiving, community, or simply keeping up with the demands of everyday life, our plates often feel overflowing. But in the middle of all the noise and necessary tasks, here's a gentle reminder: **people matter more than productivity.**

God didn't create us just to check off boxes. He created us to connect, to love, encourage, and be present with the people He's entrusted to our lives.

Now let's be clear: showing up for a friend doesn't mean rearranging your entire life or burning yourself out. It means creating intentional moments, making small but meaningful deposits of love that convey, *"You matter to me."*

Here are just a few soul-centered ways to show up with heart, not hustle:

Text a short prayer or voice note that reminds her she's seen and covered.

- Drop off her favorite treat or coffee, just because.

- Find a way to bring joy to her kids or lighten her load (sometimes loving her means loving on her family).
- Celebrate her wins, whether big or quiet, with genuine joy.
- Be the one who sits quietly with her in the hard stuff, no advice needed.

Sometimes presence speaks louder than words. As Epicurus once said: "It is not so much our friends' help that helps us, as the confidence of their help."

Let your friendships carry that kind of confidence. The kind that says, *"I may not always be there physically, but I'm with you in spirit, in prayer, and in love."*

And if you truly can't be there? Be honest. Extend grace, not guilt. A real friend will understand when your *"no" is rare* and rooted in reality, not routine, not careless, and never cold.

In this fast-paced world, your intentionality will set you apart. Time may be limited, but love is limitless when offered with sincerity. A thoughtful gesture, no matter how small, has the power to strengthen bonds, restore hearts, and reflect Christ's love in the most beautiful way.

It's the Little Things That Matter

You don't have to be a superhero to be a good friend. You don't need to have all the answers, all the time in the world, or a Pinterest-perfect way to show up. What matters most? Your heart. Your intentionality. Your presence.

Because often, it's not the grand gestures that leave the most significant impact. It's the quiet, thoughtful ones. The ones that whisper, *"You're not alone. I see you. I care."*

Try this:

- Ask, *"How are you... really?"* And then pause long enough to listen truly.
- Send a handwritten card, a coffee, or a small care package just because.
- Be the first to say, *"I'm so proud of you."* Don't assume she already knows; speak it out loud.
- Write her a simple note listing what you love, respect, or admire about her. It may become her lifeline on a hard day.
- Let her vent without rushing to fix it. Be a soft place to land, not a solution center.
- Show up when it's inconvenient, not because it's easy, but because she matters.

These may seem like small things, but when done with love, they become valuable. They carry the power to restore a weary heart, breathe life into a discouraged spirit, and deepen trust in ways words can't always explain.

Never underestimate the weight of your kindness. Sometimes the tiniest acts become the loudest echo of God's love in someone's life. So don't wait for the "perfect" moment or the "right" time, just show up in small ways. That's where real friendship lives.

Don't Just Be There, Stay There

Friendship is not just about moments, it's about consistency. Be the one she knows she can count on when:

- The baby won't stop crying.
- The diagnosis comes.
- The business flops.

- The family drama hits.
- The grief is too deep to speak about.
- The world is full of fair-weather friends. Be a storm-standing friend.

And remember... Let her be there for you, too.

Friend, you don't always have to be the strong one. Let people love you, let someone check in on you, and let your friends show up for you, too. This isn't a one-sided friendship model. We give and receive. We pour out, and we get filled up again.

A Prayer for Being a Better Friend

Lord,

Make me a woman who shows up, not out of obligation but out of love. Let me be a friend who listens, encourages, celebrates, and supports. Especially when it matters most.

Teach me to be thoughtful with my time, intentional with my words, and generous with my love. When I feel overwhelmed or unsure of how to help, remind me to ask You what I should do. Help me to remember that even small actions done in love make a big difference.

And Lord, help me receive love too; without guilt, shame, or hesitation.

In Jesus' Name, Amen.

Real Talk Reflection

1. Who in your life needs your love, support, or presence right now?
2. Is there a friend who's been there for you that you need to pause and thank?

3. What's one thing you can do today to show up for someone you love?
4. Are you setting boundaries and giving from a full, healthy heart, or from pressure or fear?
5. Have you been letting others be there for you, or have you been hiding your need?

Final Word:

It's not about having the right words. It's about having the right heart. And when you show up with love, empathy, and a spirit-led heart, you become the kind of friend everyone prays for.

The most I can do for my friend is simply be her friend.
—*Henry David Thoreau*

Commandment VIII
Keep Her Name Safe When She's Not in the Room

Who gossips with you will gossip about you. — Irish Proverb

A good name is more desirable than great riches; to be esteemed is better than silver or gold. — Proverbs 22:1, NIV

Sis, Protect Her Name and Your Own

There's one thing you carry into every room before you ever say a word: *your name.*

It speaks for you when you're not around. It precedes you in rooms you haven't entered yet. It covers your children, your household, and your legacy. So guard it like treasure. Because that's precisely what it is.

In this chapter, we're calling out a silent destroyer of relationships and reputations: *gossip.*

Gossip is sneaky. It can disguise itself as "concern," "keeping it real," or even "venting." But make no mistake, gossip is a thief. It takes away your ability to be grateful for the relationship, and whatever you're not grateful for, you usually lose. It steals peace, trust, credibility, and honor. And sis, when you participate in it, you're not just damaging someone else's name; you're ruining your own.

Gossip Is a Character Issue, Not a Personality Trait

Gossip is not cute. It's not a quirk. It's not a funny personality trait. It's a destructive pattern that says more about your own heart than the person you're talking about.

Here's the truth: If they'll gossip to you, they'll gossip about you.

That "funny" friend who always has the tea? That coworker who seems to know everybody's business but shares none of her own? That church sister who always wants to "pray" about what so-and-so is going through? Sis. ***Red flag.***

Why You've Got to Protect Your Friend's Name

A woman's name is more than just letters; it's her character, her integrity, her legacy. It carries the weight of her choices, her growth, and even the things she's still healing from. And just like you'd want your name protected in a room you're not in, your friend deserves that same covering.

A real friend is a safe place, not a secret spiller. A loyal sister doesn't entertain gossip; she silences it. A godly woman knows the *power of protection* over exposure.

If your friend trusts you with her private pain, her past, her struggles, or even her dreams, that's not casual information. That's sacred ground. You've been invited into the inner courts of her heart. You are now her vault. **Act like it.**

That means you shut down messy conversations with class. You don't repost, reframe, or retell what wasn't yours to carry publicly. You cover her not because she's perfect, but because you know what it feels like to be imperfect and still worthy of love.

Covering your friend doesn't mean enabling wrongdoing; it means refusing to be a megaphone for her missteps. It means honoring the process God has her in, even if you don't fully understand it.

Because the truth is: friendship isn't proven in the spotlight. It's proven in the shadows. When no one's watching. When no one will clap for your silence. When you protect her name, not for praise, but out of principle.

You want to be the kind of woman who can be trusted. Who keeps confidence sacred. Who honors the heart of another without question. So the next time you're tempted to share what isn't yours, remember: You're not just protecting her name; *you're protecting your own.*

Gossip is the Language of the Insecure

Let's keep it 100. People gossip when they're:

- Bored with their own lives,
- Unhappy with their own choices,
- Or distracted from their purpose.

Gossip fills a void. It gives people a false sense of power over someone else's pain. But, sis, that power is counterfeit. It'll turn on you, every time. So if you catch yourself about to spill something that isn't yours to pour, pause.

Before you speak about someone else, pause and ask yourself:

- "What in me needs attention right now?"
- "What am I avoiding in my own life?"
- "Why do I feel the need to tear someone else down?"

Sit with those questions, and then commit to healing the parts of you that need it. The energy you're spending on gossip? Redirect it toward growth. Pour that time into becoming the woman God has called and created you to be.

When your focus shifts to your own purpose, goals, and

healing, gossip naturally fades. You simply won't have time to talk about others because you'll be too busy building a life so full, so radiant, so inspiring... that it speaks for itself.

Let others talk if they must. You've got a destiny to chase and a life to create, one that you can be proud to talk about. Instead of talking about the lives of others, build a life that you want to talk about.

Choose to Cover, Not Expose

You don't have to lie. You don't have to excuse or defend what's wrong. But you do need the wisdom to know when it's time to say:

- "That's not my story to tell."
- "Let's pray for her instead."
- "I'm not comfortable talking about that."
- "That's between them and God."

You can always choose love. You can always choose to cover your friend with grace instead of exposing her with judgment.

And yes, beautiful friend, you can always choose silence. Because sometimes, silence is wisdom. Sometimes, silence becomes a powerful choice that protects more than words ever could. Many times, silence speaks louder than gossip ever could. In the right moment, silence becomes a sacred shield, protecting your friend, your peace, your heart, and your friendship.

Above all, love each other deeply, because love covers over a multitude of sins. —1 Peter 4:8 (NIV)

Reputation: Protect It Like It's Gold

Proverbs 22:1 says, "A good name is more desirable than great riches." Your name is your brand. Your reputation is your witness. Your character is your currency in this world. Don't sell it cheap for likes, laughs, gossip, or false sisterhood.

Ask yourself:

1. Would I want this revealed or verbally repeated about me?
2. Would I be okay if my child heard me say or saw me do this?
3. Am I honoring God, my sister, and myself with these words or actions?

Your name, and how you speak about other people's names, matters.

What If You're the One Being Talked About?

If you're the target of gossip, *pause, breathe.*

- Don't feed the fire.
- Don't match energy.
- Don't start a gossip war in return.

Instead, stand tall in your truth. Make sure your truth and your life is something you can be proud of. If they're not, spend your time and energy rebuilding.

Address the gossip in love if needed. And then release it. Remember that God is your defender, and your consistent integrity and life that you're building will speak louder than any rumor ever could.

Whatever you are currently doing, will eventually result

in a harvest based on the type of seed you decide to sow whether someone is gossiping about you right now or not. So stop worrying, keep working, and trust God.

But the Lord defends me; my God protects me.
—Psalm 94:22, GNT

...for the battle is the Lord's, and He will give you into our hands. —1 Samuel 17:47, NKJV

Fear not, for I am with you; be not dismayed, for I am your God; I will strengthen you, I will help you, I will uphold you with my righteous right hand. —Isaiah 41:10, ESV

A Prayer to Guard My Mouth and Protect My Sister

Father,

Help me guard my tongue and protect the names of others with love and loyalty. Give me the wisdom to know when to speak and the strength to stay silent when I need to. Make me a safe place for my sisters, a vault for their stories, and a reflection of Your grace. Let me build up, not tear down. Use my words to heal, to bless, and to honor Your name.

In Jesus' Name, Amen.

Reflection Time

1. Who have I spoken about that I need to apologize to?
2. What conversation have I entertained that I should've shut down?
3. Am I known as someone who gossips… or someone who guards?

4. Do I protect my sisters' names and reputations the way I want mine protected?
5. What kind of legacy am I building with the words I speak?

Final Word, Sis...

You don't have to be perfect. But you do need to be intentional. Let your name carry weight, not because of popularity but because of integrity.

Let people say:

- "She doesn't play about people's names."
- "She shuts down gossip with class and kindness."
- "If you told her, it stayed with her."

That's who you are. That's the kind of friend God is calling you to be. And when you protect her name, you're also preserving your own.

Live so that you wouldn't be ashamed to sell the family parrot to the town gossip. —Will Rogers

Commandment IX
Listen to Hear, Not to Respond

The most called-upon prerequisite of a friend is an accessible ear.
— Maya Angelou

God gave us two ears and one mouth for a reason: so we would listen twice as much as we speak.
— Epictetus (paraphrased)

Real Friendship Requires Real Listening

How often are we truly listening to each other?

Not the distracted, half-present kind of listening where you're nodding while scrolling...
Not the "Mmm-hmm, girl" while mentally crafting your own response...
Not the quick fix-it or "let me one-up your story" kind of reply.

We're talking about soul-deep, silent listening. The kind that pauses, leans in, and says without a word: "I see you. I hear you. I'm here."
In a world full of noise, opinions, and endless notifications, listening has become a rare gift. And because it's rare, it's all the more powerful. It's healing. It's holy.

Sometimes, your friend doesn't need advice. She doesn't need a Bible verse. She doesn't need a solution. She just needs space to feel. To be. To breathe.

And when you slow down long enough to give her that space, something beautiful happens. Trust is built. Walls come down. Connection takes root. Because when a woman feels heard, she feels held.

Jesus was a master listener. He didn't just hear words; He heard hearts. He modeled a kind of presence we're all craving today: one that's undistracted, fully present, and grounded in love.

So let's follow His lead. Let's be the kind of friend who listens with our whole heart, not to respond, but to understand. Because in true sisterhood, the ministry of presence is often more powerful than the ministry of words.

Stop Listening to Respond. Start Listening to Understand.

Active listening isn't about being quiet until it's your turn to talk. It's about making space emotionally, mentally, and spiritually for someone else's thoughts and feelings.

When you truly listen:

1. You silence your inner commentary.
2. You lay down the need to be right or to fix it.
3. You stop centering yourself in a moment that doesn't belong to you.

It's not just about giving advice. It's about giving presence. And that presence might be the exact healing balm your sister needs.

Silence Is Sacred

Speech is silver, but silence is golden. — Proverb

The friend who can be silent with us in a moment of despair... is a friend who cares. — Henri Nouwen

There will be moments in friendship when words fall short. When pain is too raw. When answers are unclear. When grief or anxiety has tangled her thoughts, and all she can offer is a heavy sigh or quiet tears.

In those moments, **don't reach for the perfect thing to say. Just be.** Sit beside her. Stay present. Be still. Let the silence speak love in ways your words never could.

Let her cry without hurrying her healing. Let her ramble without correcting her emotions. Let her sit in confusion without rushing in with clarity. Let her be, while you simply stay.

You are not her Savior. You're her sister. You don't have to fix what God is still unfolding. Your job is to stand near while He does the healing.

In a world that rushes to speak, the gift of quiet presence is rare and valuable. Sometimes the greatest comfort you can give is not in your advice, but in your availability. Your steady hand. Your gentle nod. Your willingness to hold space without trying to fill it.

Because real friendship knows: Sometimes love sounds like silence. And sometimes healing begins with someone simply sitting beside you, without needing to rescue you. Learn how to be the calm, not the commentary.

Why Listening Matters

Listening is how trust is built. It's how hearts open. It's

how emotional safety is established. It's how you discern who's really in front of you, what their intentions are, how they move, and what they need.

Here's the truth: People will tell you exactly who they are, what they need, and what they value if you'll just stop talking long enough to listen. It's not just about strengthening your friendships. It's how you protect your heart. When you truly listen, you see people clearly before you overextend yourself emotionally, physically, or spiritually.

Listening Is How You Love

You can't love someone well if you don't know them. And you can't truly know them if you're always the one filling the space. Real love begins with listening, not just with your ears, but with your heart.

It's in the curious questions you ask, not to pry, but to understand. It's in the way you lean in when their voice falters. It's in how you notice the little things: the slight change in their tone, the way their shoulders sag when they say, "I'm fine," or how their eyes dart when they're holding back tears.

Sometimes, what matters most isn't what they say. It's what they don't say. It's what they're too tired, too guarded, or too unsure to put into words.

And if you're truly present, not distracted, not halfway there, you'll catch it. You'll feel the nudge in your spirit that says, *"Ask again. Stay a little longer. Lean in with grace."*

Because listening isn't passive, it's one of the most active, intentional, and sacred ways you can show love.

As Dave Tyson Gentry once said: "True friendship comes when the silence between two people is comfortable."

Let's be women who don't rush to respond or even give wisdom, but who pause, notice, and care deeply. Because sometimes the most profound love isn't loud, it's quiet. It's present. It's paying attention.

To listen well is to love well. And that kind of love? It changes everything.

Practice the Pause

The next time your friend is sharing, don't rush to respond. Pause. Let her words breathe. Let her feel safe enough to go deeper. And if you do speak, make sure your words are soft, wise, and anchored in compassion...not assumption.

Sometimes, your best response will be:

- "Tell me more."
- "How did that make you feel?"
- "What do you need right now?"
- "I'm so sorry you're carrying this."

No solutions. No preaching. Just love.

Let Your Body Listen Too

Listening isn't just something you do; it's something your whole self participates in. Long before you speak a word, your body is already having a conversation. And in friendship, that nonverbal presence can be the very thing that makes someone feel truly seen, safe, and supported.

Because your body speaks love in ways your mouth sometimes can't.

- Eye contact says, "You matter to me. I'm here with you."
- A gentle nod says, "I hear you. Keep going."

- Putting the phone down says, "You have my full attention."
- Silence says, "I'm making space for your voice. I don't need to fill it."

And when words feel too far away or too heavy to find, it's okay to just sit with her. No advice. No fixing. No performance. Your presence is more powerful than you think.

Sometimes the healing begins not when you say the perfect thing, but when you simply choose to stay, to be fully there in body, mind, and spirit. That kind of presence is rare. That kind of presence is special. So let your body become a safe haven. A mirror of God's love. A message that says: *"I'm not rushing you. I'm not judging you. I'm not distracted. I'm here, and you're not alone."*

Listening Builds New Friendships Too

Want to build deeper, more meaningful relationships? Start by doing something rare: *genuinely care about someone else's story.*

In a world where everyone is busy performing, trying to impress, prove, or keep up, connection often gets lost in the noise. But you, sister, have the power to shift the atmosphere by doing something beautifully simple: *listen with intention.*

The next time you meet someone new, don't lead with your résumé. Don't rush to be interesting. Just be interested.

- Ask a thoughtful question.
- Compliment something real, not just their outfit, but their energy, their courage, their kindness.
- Pause long enough to let them share, and then stay

long enough to let them feel seen.

That one moment of kindness, that choice to slow down and listen, might be the first time someone has felt truly heard in weeks... maybe even months. And that's how beautiful, soul-deep friendships begin, not with big gestures or perfect words, but with quiet presence and compassionate curiosity.

Because at the heart of every strong friendship is the simple truth: *"You matter. Your story matters. I'm listening."*

So go ahead, be that woman. The one who doesn't just talk well but listens deeply. The one who builds bridges, not walls. The one who turns strangers into sisters through the sacred art of paying attention.

Friendship doesn't start with impressing. It starts with intentional listening.

5 Soul-Opening Questions to Spark Authentic Connection

These questions aren't about being nosy; they're about creating space for honesty, vulnerability, and soul-level bonding. Use them gently. Ask with warmth. Listen without judgment. And let the conversation unfold with grace.

1. *"What's something you're carrying right now that most people wouldn't know just by looking at you?"*

This question gently opens the door for honesty without pressure. It lets her know she's allowed to be real, and that you're safe enough to hear it.

2. *"What's been bringing you joy lately, big or small?"*

This question focuses on celebration, reminding her to look for the light even in the heaviest seasons. It gives you insight into what fills her soul.

3. "What's something you've overcome that's made you stronger?"

This invites her to share a piece of her story with dignity and pride. It shifts the conversation from surface-level to sacred ground.

4. "When do you feel most like yourself?"

This is a beautiful way to learn what gives her life, identity, and freedom. It shows you care about who she really is, not just who she appears to be.

5. "What do you need more of in this season: grace, rest, courage, or support?"

This question serves as a gentle check-in, conveying compassion and intention. Sometimes, just being asked this question can bring healing.

Pro Tip: Don't rush her answers. Let silence breathe. Let her find her words. And respond with presence, not performance. Deep friendships are built in the quiet spaces between questions and answers.

Reflection Questions

1. How often do I slow down to truly listen to those around me?
2. Am I more focused on my response than their feel-

ings?
3. Who in my life do I need to pause and really listen to?
4. What is my body language saying when someone is talking to me?
5. When was the last time I listened and didn't try to "fix" something?

A Prayer for Listening Hearts

God,

Help me to quiet my thoughts, still my responses, and open my heart to listen well. Let my ears be tuned to the people You've placed in my life. Help me to listen not with judgment but with compassion. Not to fix, but to hold space. Not to respond but to understand. Make me a friend who listens deeply, speaks wisely, and loves like You.

In Jesus' Name, Amen.

Final Word, Sis…

You don't have to have all the answers. You don't need perfect advice. You just need to show up with your ears open and your heart engaged. When you become the kind of friend who listens, you become the kind of friend people remember forever. Because we may forget the words people say…But we'll never forget how deeply heard we felt in their presence.

Silence makes the real conversations between friends. Not the saying, but the never needing to say that counts.
- Margaret Lee Runbeck

Commandment X
Apologize Often, Forgive Freely

You can always tell a real friend: when you've made a fool of yourself, they don't feel you've done a permanent job.
— Laurence J. Peter

To a friend's house, the road is never long.
— Danish Proverb

When Life Gets Messy

Friendship is one of life's greatest gifts, but even the most beautiful friendships will be tested because life gets messy. And so do we.

We're human. We hurt each other, even when we don't mean to. We misunderstand, misstep, and misspeak. We get tired. We grow in different directions. We carry baggage. We get triggered by old wounds.

But it's not the mess that determines the strength of a friendship. It's what we choose to do in the middle of it.

Do we ghost each other out of pride or fear? Do we let hurt fester in silence until the friendship quietly dies? Do we wear resentment like armor, convincing ourselves we were right, even if it costs us connection?

Or…Do we take the higher road? The one paved with grace, humility, courage, and healing?

Because **real friendship will require forgiveness.** Again and again. It will stretch us to grow past offense. It will invite us to have hard conversations instead of harboring hidden hurts. It will call us to love through the awkward, the uncomfortable, the inconvenient.

And when we forgive, not just with our words, but with our hearts, something divine happens.

To forgive is to set a prisoner free and discover the prisoner was you.
—Lewis B. Smedes

Sometimes the breakthrough in your friendship isn't about who was right. It's about who's willing to go first: to say, "Let's talk. Let's try. Let's heal."

Grace doesn't excuse the wound, but it creates the space for restoration. Forgiveness doesn't mean forgetting; it means choosing your freedom over bitterness. And freedom is always worth fighting for.

Why Forgiveness Matters, Even Though It's Hard

In all honesty, forgiveness *is* hard. It asks you to rise higher. To lay down your right to feel justified. To release someone who may never say, "I was wrong." It asks you to surrender the mental replay reel, the conversations, the hurt, the injustice, and trust that God saw it all. It requires you to remember:

Beloved, never avenge yourselves, but leave the way open for God's wrath {and His judicial righteousness}; for it is written {in Scripture}, "Vengeance is Mine, I will repay," —Romans 12:19, AMP

And hear this, sis: **Forgiveness is not weakness.** It's spiritual strength. It's emotional maturity. It's the sacred decision to protect your peace and choose freedom over bitterness.

Forgiveness doesn't mean pretending the pain never happened. It means refusing to let it have power over your future. It's saying, **"God, I trust You to handle what I can't.** I'm releasing this, not because they deserve it, but because I deserve peace. And I know that if I put this and them in Your hands, You will cover me with perfect peace."

You will keep in perfect and constant peace the one whose mind is steadfast {that is, committed and focused on You—in both inclination and character}, because he trusts and takes refuge in You {with hope and confident expectation}. —Isaiah 26:3, AMP

For I know the plans and thoughts that I have for you,' says the Lord, 'plans for peace and well-being and not for disaster, to give you a future and a hope. —Jeremiah 29:11, AMP

When you choose to forgive:

- You pull up the root of resentment from your own heart.
- You reclaim the peace the enemy tried to steal.
- You make room for joy, clarity, blessings, and new beginnings.

And the truth is, the longer you hold on, the heavier it gets. The faster you forgive, the faster you can move forward.

Forgiveness isn't letting them off the hook. It's taking yourself off the hook of bitterness. It's releasing a weight that was never meant to be yours to carry. **You weren't the one who did wrong,** but you can be the one who chooses to heal. You can put the pain down. Lay it on God's altar.

Let it go. And step boldly into the bright, beautiful future that's waiting for you on the other side of surrender.

Resentment is like drinking poison and waiting for the other person to die. —Nelson Mandela

So today, let it go. Not for them. For you. Because your future is too important, your peace is too precious. And the plans God has for you are too good to be delayed by what should've been, could've been, or never was.

When You've Caused Hurt, Take the First Step Back

Sis, can we talk heart to heart? If you've hurt someone, even if it wasn't on purpose, be woman enough, be healed enough, and be wise enough to own it. Apologize. Not with a defense. Not with a disclaimer. Not with a "but you..." at the end.

Just. Apologize.

With humility, say, "I was wrong." "I'm truly sorry." "I didn't mean to hurt you, but I now understand that I did."

That kind of honesty? That kind of spirit-led maturity? It's healing oil. It softens walls that pride has built up over time. It speaks to the heart that thought you didn't care, and it reminds people that real love is still alive in this world.

The Bible says, "Confess your faults one to another, and pray for one another, that ye may be healed", James 5:16, KJV. Do you see the beauty in that? Healing comes in the honesty. Wholeness begins when we choose humility over ego.

As an empowerment and relationship coach, I often remind others: Apologizing isn't weakness, it's leadership. It takes strength to say, "I was wrong." It takes courage to admit, "I missed it." And it takes emotional maturity to say,

"I hurt you, and I want to do better."

Owning your actions isn't a sign of failure, it's a reflection of growth, responsibility, and love. You don't need a long speech. You just need a clean heart and a sincere mouth. Whether the relationship is restored or not, your peace is tied to your obedience to God, not the outcome. And sometimes, that one act of humility can mend years of damage. It can breathe new life into a friendship that still has purpose written all over it.

A real friend is one who walks in when the rest of the world walks out. — Walter Winchell

So, if that's who you want to be, start by walking back in...with truth, grace, and love leading the way.

Real Friends May Hurt Eachother...and Still Choose Each-other

Real talk, when a stranger wrongs you, you can brush it off. But when someone you've laughed with, prayed with, and shared secrets with...when they hurt you? That's a different kind of ache. That's the kind of pain that sits deep.

And yet, don't miss this...even the most authentic, loving friendships will go through moments of disappointment. Why? Because we are human. Because we are flawed. Because we're learning, growing, and trying to love each other well while still healing ourselves.

But here's the beauty: the deepest roots of friendship often grow in those moments of tension, truth-telling, and tearful reconnection.

The Bible reminds us in Proverbs 27:6, "Faithful are the wounds of a friend…"

That verse may sound uncomfortable at first, but it

holds deep truth. A real friend won't always tell you what you want to hear, she'll tell you what you need to hear. Not to harm you, but to help you. Her words may sting in the moment, but they are meant to stretch you, grow you, and bring you back to truth.

A faithful friend isn't afraid to lovingly call you higher. She won't cosign your dysfunction or celebrate what's unhealthy just to keep the peace. And when you're that kind of friend in return, you'll learn to value correction as an act of love, not criticism.

And here's the beautiful part: a real friend won't leave you after a hard moment. She'll stay. She'll choose you again, even when the conversation was uncomfortable or the truth was hard to swallow. And you'll choose her too. Because friendship isn't forged in the "easy"...*it's proven in the fire.*

True sisterhood is built in those refining moments; the ones that test your loyalty, stretch your patience, and deepen your love. So yes, fight for your friendship when it's worth it and not toxic. But fight with love, not ego. Fight with humility, not pride. Don't come to prove your point; come to protect the connection.

Friendship that endures through honest conversations, missteps, and mutual grace? That's gold. That's the kind of friendship we pray for. That's the kind of friend we strive to be.

How to Repair What's Broken

Sometimes we're the ones who cause the wound. We said the wrong thing. We acted out of fear, pride, or pain. We didn't show up when it mattered, or maybe we did, but not in the way they needed us to.

And when that happens, it can feel easier to avoid the conversation than to face the discomfort. But healing begins with honesty, and it grows through humility.

So, if you've made a mistake, don't hide. Don't excuse it. Don't wait for things to "blow over."

Face it with maturity, compassion, and courage. Say what needs to be said. Own what needs to be owned. Don't minimize the impact just because you didn't intend to cause harm. And then, give them the space to heal.

You can't rush someone else's process. You can't demand forgiveness or dictate the timeline of reconciliation. **When you've caused hurt, you don't get to decide when the conversation happens or how long it should last.** But you can choose how you show up, with softness, patience, and grace.

Leave the door open, without pressure. If they return, that's beautiful. If they don't, you'll still know you did your part.

You showed up with love instead of pride. You offered peace instead of pretending. And whether or not the friendship is restored, you grew into a woman who repairs instead of retreats.

The manner in which your relationships end will determine the health of your relationships going forward.
—Marla A. McCarthy

Sometimes the restoration isn't found in getting the relationship back; it's found in how you handled the ending. When you choose wisdom over pride, humility over blame, and peace over pettiness, you're not just closing a chapter; you're preparing your heart for something or someone better.

How you end this season will shape how you begin the next one.

The Ten Commandments Of Friendship

If You've Been Hurt...

Not all friendship wounds are created equal. Some are misunderstandings. Others are patterns. Some are forgivable missteps. Others are signs it's time to draw a hard line.

When you've been hurt, take a moment to pause and ask yourself:

1. Was this intentional or unintentional?
2. Is this a pattern or a one-time moment?
3. Does this friend genuinely love me, but simply missed the mark?

One painful moment doesn't always mean the friendship is broken. But repeated disregard, manipulation, or emotional neglect may point to something deeper: toxic dynamics that need to be addressed or released.

Sometimes, we're called to offer grace, the same kind of grace we hope others would extend to us when we fall short. Other times, we're called to set clear, healthy boundaries with those who consistently dishonor our time, values, or well-being.

Letting go doesn't always mean cutting someone off. It may simply mean **redefining the space they occupy in your life.** Not everyone deserves front-row access to your heart. And that's not bitterness, it's wisdom.

In some cases, walking away is love:

- Love for your own peace and well-being.
- Love for your mental and emotional health.
- Love for the woman you're becoming and the life you're building.

Holding on out of guilt, fear, or nostalgia can keep you

tethered to pain. But choosing to honor yourself and trusting God with the rest is an act of spiritual maturity.

You can forgive and still move forward. You can release someone in love and still keep your peace. Discernment is key. And grace? Grace is still required, for them and for you.

End Well, Even If It Ends

Not every relationship will last forever. And that's okay. But if you have to walk away, do it with your dignity. Do it with forgiveness in your heart. And do it in a way that you'll be proud of five or ten years from now.

Don't burn bridges. Don't slam doors. Don't let bitterness write the last chapter. Leave space for healing. You never know what time, growth, and grace may bring back around.

10 Gentle Steps for Healing Friendship Wounds

1. Address it: Be honest. Don't pretend it didn't hurt if it did.
2. Keep it private : Correct in private. Never humiliate publicly.
3. Listen: Truly listen to their side. You might be surprised.
4. Consider your flaws: You're not perfect either. The need for forgiveness and grace goes both ways.
5. Reminisce: Recall what made the friendship special.
6. Prioritize your health: Release resentment and all negative emotions. It's toxic to your spirit.
7. Set boundaries: Moving forward with wisdom is self-care.
8. Avoid drama: Say what needs to be said, then release it.

9. Forgive even without apology: It's for your own freedom, not theirs.
10. Move on with peace: Life is too full of possibilities and purpose to live in the past.

How to Ask for Forgiveness Gracefully

- **Listen first:** Let them say how they feel, even if it hurts.
- **Apologize sincerely:** No excuses. Just truth and love.
- **Explain** (if needed): Share your heart, not just your words.
- **Be accountable:** Own it. Every part of it.
- **Give space:** Let them heal without pressure.
- **Do Better:** Let your actions speak louder than your apology.

When asking for forgiveness and hoping to remain a part of someone's life, it's not just about saying the right words; **it's about showing real and lasting change.** True transformation is proven over time, through a renewed mindset and consistent, loving behavior. Let your changed behavior speak for you. Let the way you live reflect the sincerity of your request.

Reflection Questions:

1. Who have I hurt, intentionally or unintentionally?
2. Who do I need to apologize to today?
3. Who hurt me that I'm still holding onto?
4. What's one step I can take to let go and be free?
5. What is the most loving way to handle this situation?

6. Am I more committed to being "right" or being at peace?
7. Is there a friendship I want to restore? What's stopping me?

A Prayer for Healing and Restoration

Lord,

Give me the strength to forgive those who've hurt me and the humility to apologize when I've hurt others. Help me release what no longer serves me and hold tightly to what is sacred and true. Let love guide my responses, grace guide my heart, and wisdom guide my next steps. I trust You to heal what's broken and to restore what's meant to be.

In Jesus' Name, Amen.

Final Word, Sis…

Life moves fast. Days blur. Seasons change. And before we know it, opportunities to love well can slip right through our fingers.

But real friendship? That's rare and special. And it's far too precious to lose over unspoken hurt, silent pride, or stubborn misunderstandings.

So be the woman who leans in. The one who's quick to listen, quicker to forgive, and strong enough to say, "I was wrong." Not because you're weak, but because you know that reconciliation is stronger and more valuable than ego.

Friendship was never about perfection; it was always about commitment. Commitment to keep showing up. To offer grace even when it's hard. To grow through the awkward, the uncomfortable, and the messy. To love each other back to wholeness when life breaks us down.

The Ten Commandments Of Friendship

Always remember:

There is nothing on this earth more to be prized than true friendship. —Thomas Aquinas

Hold a true friend with both your hands. —Nigerian Proverb

So here's your reminder, sis: Good friendships don't just happen; they're nurtured. Tend to your friendships like the sacred gardens they are. Pull the weeds. Water them with kindness. Protect what's blooming. And never be afraid to repair what's worth saving.

Sometimes, repair means starting over, pulling up everything, and starting anew.. Retilling the ground, nourishing the soil, planting new seeds, and then doing the hard but holy work of waiting.

Patiently trusting that God will breathe on those seeds and cause them to grow. Water your friendships and your life with His Word. Speak life. Stay soft. Do the work. Because in a world full of noise, shallow connections, and fast goodbyes, real friendship is still a divine gift. It's worth the tending. It's worth the fight. So when you find it, fight to keep it.

Conclusion

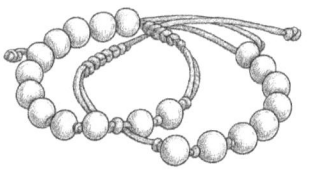

Sis, you made it! You've journeyed through *The Ten Commandments of Friendship: Sisterhood Principles Every Woman Should Live By*, and I couldn't be more proud of you. Not just for reading but for daring to reflect, to grow, and to love better.

You've now been equipped with a full blueprint for building, healing, and nurturing strong, lasting, godly friendships. You've learned how to:

- Choose wisely who deserves access to your heart.
- Speak life, not gossip.
- Set boundaries without guilt.
- Celebrate your friends' wins as if they were your own.
- Forgive with grace.
- Apologize with humility.
- Listen with your heart, not just your ears.
- Show up when it matters most.
- Most importantly, we should love deeply and authentically, just as God loves us.

These are not just tips, they are transformational truths. And when you begin to live by them, your life, the energy you give off, and who you attract will change.

Why This Book Matters

Too many women are lonely, guarded, and isolated, not because we don't want friendship, but because no one may have ever taught us how to be true friends. That's what this book is here to do. Whether you've been burned before or you're yearning to go deeper with the women in your life, these commandments are your compass.

Friendships don't have to be complicated, competitive, or cold. They can be beautiful, warm, safe, soul-deep, and life-giving. They can reflect heaven. They can be filled with the love of God. But first, someone has to show others the way.

You are that someone.

Make This a Movement

This book wasn't written just for you; it was written for your sisters, your daughters, your small group, your besties, and the women you haven't even met yet.

Imagine what would happen if we all learned to love each other better. What would change in our homes, our churches, our communities…and in ourselves?

Let's not stop here. Let's make this a movement.

Here's What You Can Do Next:

1. Share this book. Gift one to your best friend, your mother, your sister, your daughter, your coworkers, or the women in your church and community. Real transformation happens when we journey together.
2. Host a Book Club or Girls' Night In. Use *The Ten Commandments of Friendship: Sisterhood Principles Every Woman Should Live By* as the foundation for a life-giving

discussion or monthly gathering. There's power in sisterhood.
3. Gift and use this book in your next retreat, conference, or workshop.

Whether you're a women's group or ministry leader, life coach, or simply passionate about uplifting women, these ten commandments make the perfect structure for:

- Friendship workshops
- Women's conferences
- Healing circles
- Small group Bible studies
- Teen girl mentoring
- Women's wellness retreats

4. Partner with the author. Want a virtual or in-person speaker to bring these truths to life at your event? Let's collaborate! Use the contact information at the back of the book or website to reach out.

You Are A Critical Part of the Movement

If led to do so, take 60 seconds to leave a heartfelt review wherever books are sold online (Amazon, Barnes & Noble, etc.). Your words can inspire another woman to take the leap into real healing and connection.

Remember to post your favorite quote from the book on social media, tag us using #10CommandmentsOfFriendship, and follow along for future resources, events, and encouragement.

Let's Stay Connected

This isn't goodbye, this is just the beginning. If you haven't already, visit MarlaMcCarthy.com and momlifewithmarla.com and join our online community. You'll have access to exclusive resources, retreat invites, printables, coaching information, and upcoming book releases.

And if you're on Instagram, come say hi at @momlifewithmarla. I'd love to hear what chapter resonated most with you!

Final Thoughts

Real, healthy, lasting friendship is not a myth. It's a miracle...but it's one you can be part of.

Start small. Start now. Start with yourself. Be the kind of friend that God would smile down on. Be the friend that lifts others higher. Be the friend who speaks life, shows up, listens deeply, and forgives freely.

If you commit to following the wisdom of these ten commandments, you won't just change your friendships, you'll change your life.

From my heart to yours...Thank you for reading, for seeking wisdom, for loving, and for showing up. Let's keep building this sisterhood one powerful friendship at a time.

With love and a heart full of gratitude,
~ *Marla*

About the Author

Marla McCarthy is a passionate voice for women, moms, and sisterhood. A devoted wife of over 25 years, loving mother of seven, and certified Master Empowerment and Relationship Coach, Marla brings both wisdom and real-life experience to everything she writes, teaches, and shares. Her heart beats for women who are ready to break free from isolation, heal from past hurts and betrayal, to build deep, meaningful, and lasting connections.

With a natural ability to combine faith, humor, truth, and encouragement, Marla empowers women to embrace who they are, walk in their God-given identity, and show up boldly in their friendships, families, and purpose. Her words feel like a hug, her advice feels like a warm cup of tea, and her heart is as big as Texas (where she proudly lives, loves, and serves).

Marla is the founder of Mom Life with Marla, an online community that inspires busy moms and women to create the life they truly want, one filled with faith, fulfillment, and real connection. Whether she's teaching on stage, mentoring women, writing books or devotionals, or leading transformational retreats, her mission is the same: to help women heal, connect, and grow into the best version of themselves, together.

In *The Ten Commandments of Friendship: Sisterhood Principles Every Woman Should Live By,* Marla shares the very principles that have helped her build and maintain beautiful, soul-deep friendships through every season of life. She believes friendship is valuable, sisterhood is powerful, and healing is always possible.

Connect with Marla for booking, workshops, retreats, or event inquiries: www.momlifewithmarla.com, www.MarlaMcCarthy.com, and on Instagram: @momlifewithmarla

ALSO AVAILABLE FROM
THE REAL LIFE SERIES PUBLISHING CO.

Enhancing Your Journey:
90-Day Prayer Journal
by Marla A. McCarthy
ASIN: B0F37TRD72
Available at Amazon.com

Enhancing Your Journey:
A Biblical Guide To A More Powerful Prayer Life
by Marla A. McCarthy
ISBN: 979-8-9989754-3-1

Create The Life You Want:
Your 90-Day Roadmap to Purpose, Balance, and Success
by Marla A. McCarthy
ISBN: 979-8-9989754-2-4

Create The Life You Want:
90-Day Goal Journal
by Marla A. McCarthy
ASIN: B0F4W9YRP7
Available at Amazon.com

Loving Me:
A Guide To Renewing Your Mind, Body & Spirit
by Marla A. McCarthy
ISBN: 979-8-9989754-5-5

Be a Seed:
Grow Deep. Rise Strong. Multiply Good
by Marla A. McCarthy
ISBN: 979-8-9989754-6-2

www.ingramcontent.com/pod-product-compliance
Lightning Source LLC
Chambersburg PA
CBHW020550030426
42337CB00013B/1032